CHARLES TYSON YERKES
THE TRACTION
KING OF LONDON

CHARLES TYSON YERKES

THE TRACTION KING OF LONDON

TIM SHERWOOD

TEMPUS

Front cover images:
Above left: Yerkes towards the end of his life. (London Transport Museum. 1998/52441)
Above right: Photograph of Emilie Grigsby, taken in about 1900. (Courtesy of New York Public Library)
Below: The fruits of Yerkes' labours, posed at North Ealing on the Ealing and South Harrow Railway in 1903. (London Transport Museum. 1998/8744)

First published 2008

Tempus Publishing
The History Press Ltd.
Cirencester Road, Chalford,
Stroud, Gloucestershire, GL6 8PE
www.thehistorypress.co.uk

Tempus Publishing is an imprint of The History Press Ltd.

British Library Cataloguing in Publication Data.
A catalogue record for this book is available from the British Library.

ISBN 978 0 7524 4622 6

Typesetting and origination by The History Press Ltd.
Printed in Great Britain

CONTENTS

ACKNOWLEDGEMENTS

Much of the groundwork for this book was prepared at the London Transport Museum as part of an internal project. A draft has been read by Mike Ashworth and I have pleasure in thanking him for his advice; also Martin Coppins who read a draft.

I am very grateful to Eve Baker who read the final draft. My thanks to Oliver Green for generously giving permission to use material from the London Transport Museum's picture collection, Hugh Robertson for producing the pictures, and Helen Kent for assistance in the Museum's Library.

I would like to thank the staff of the National Archives, the House of Lords Record Office, the British Library, the British Library Newspaper Collection at Colindale, the London Metropolitan Archives, the City of Westminster Archives, the Guildhall Library (City of London), Richmond upon Thames Library, Kensington Central Library, the library at the University of Georgetown, Washington D.C., and Putney Library. Finally, I am extremely grateful to my friend and photographer Bruce Rankin for continual help and assistance, and especially for photographing the site of Yerkes' mansion on Fifth Avenue, New York. Needless to say any blunders are my responsibility.

INTRODUCTION

'. . . the grandest robber-baron Chicago had ever seen, a five-star, aged-in-oak, 100-proof bastard.'[1]

This is the story of Charles Tyson Yerkes, whose name is pronounced as in 'turkeys'. He lived from 1837 to 1905; his public life was controversial and colourful and his private life was astonishing. He made a fortune in Philadelphia – which he lost when he was imprisoned for fraud – and then a bigger fortune in Chicago. The leading-edge technology of his time was electrical engineering (as computers are today) and his speciality was financing tramways and urban railways by methods that were dishonest, even by the standards of the 1880s and 1890s – the American 'gilded age'. He became known as the 'Traction King', who created the 'Traction Tangle' – a concoction of dodgy construction companies, dubious holding companies, and rapacious operating companies. He spent prodigious sums on bribing politicians in order to get leases until public opinion turned on him. Then, under threats of civic violence, he was, to his surprise, driven out of the city. He was the classic robber baron[2] and came to London in 1900. Why?

London's transport was archaic, yet Yerkes was greeted with hostility in traditional financial and railway circles; this was illogical because nobody else could do anything about the paralysis. Yerkes was a wily manipulator who knew a lot about urban transport and the new field of electrification. He succeeded in funding the electrification and modernisation of the District railway, which he rightly wanted to amalgamate with the Metropolitan. He constructed the tubes which developed into the Northern, Piccadilly, and Bakerloo lines. He bought up the largest tram company, London United, and built the biggest power station in Europe. All this was done by evading parliamentary scrutiny and setting up registered holding companies. Although he did not achieve the rational, but impossible, goal of unifying the network in the Edwardian era, he laid the foundations of the Underground Group which formed the core of the London Passenger Transport Board in 1933.

To this day he arouses strong feelings, one recent writer calling his legacy 'disastrous'.[3] This view overlooks the inescapable question as to who else could have electrified the District railway and built three tube railways. As another writer put it in the 1920s, Yerkes '. . . saved the railway situation in London.'[4]

Instead of resting on his laurels and enjoying the $20 million he had plundered from Chicago, Yerkes hoped to make a third fortune in London and join the top rank of robber barons. He was encouraged to come to London by his ambitious young mistress, Emilie Grigsby, who wanted to break into Edwardian society, having been rejected by polite society in New York. A woman of legendary beauty, she had a dark secret and Londoners are in her debt. Although Yerkes had to moderate his business methods, his uninhibited private life continued in London where he juggled sexual liaisons with Emilie and three other women – apart from his wife who lived in their vast mansion in New York and periodically travelled to Europe. He went as far as paying a gigolo to keep her out of his way. Yerkes suppressed much of this during his lifetime but details seeped out after his death.

The story of Yerkes is the story of the American invasion of Britain. Although still politically unimportant, the American economy had outstripped Britain, and the story of electrification is the story of the start of American technological superiority. After a period of unprecedented economic growth – the 'Gilded Age' – America had accumulated capital which was looking for investment; Britain was a natural home.[5]

A journalist and novelist in Chicago, Theodore Dreiser, was fascinated by Yerkes and his ruthlessness, and wrote three novels based on his life. There is more about them in Appendix F. Dreiser interviewed people who had met Yerkes, and collected a large number of newspaper reports, notes and so on. The archive containing this material is held by the University of Pennsylvania. The problem for the biographer is that Yerkes committed little to writing – no diary, no memoirs etc. Some letters survived him but were, as so often happens, destroyed by his family. It is possible that Yerkes, who was highly numerate, did not possess well-honed writing skills, though his published letters in *The Times* and his report on progress of 28 April 1903 were grammatical and fluent. It is most likely that he dictated them to his secretary, Louis Owsely, who would then have composed them.

Three American historians, Philip L. Gerber, Robert Forrey, and Sydney Roberts, have published carefully researched articles about aspects of the Yerkes story and this corpus has been an invaluable source for this book. A biography was published in 2006 by the University of Illinois called *The Robber Baron*, written by John Franch. What I am offering here is no more than an interim biography that contains little of the inner man, but a critical assessment of Yerkes' contribution to the development of London's transport is overdue.

A brief word on the problem of electrification will be helpful for the reader.[6] Because streets and roads in the USA were badly surfaced, buses were not a possibility. Towns therefore relied on trams, or street railways as they were called, and they covered significant distances. There was a strong incentive to replace horse traction with something cheaper (horse feed being expensive), and the breakthrough came in 1888 when the inventor Frank Sprague (see note 42 on page 39) opened an electric tramway at Richmond, Virginia. Two manufacturers of electrical equipment emerged: General Electric and Westinghouse. At the Chicago World Exhibition of 1893, General Electric installed a short section of electric railway. Two years later General Electric electrified the Metropolitan Elevated Railway at Chicago, followed by the South Side Elevated two years after that, in 1897. By this time both General Electric and Westinghouse had equipped most American street railways and started looking abroad for orders. Clearly, expertise had been accumulated that did not yet exist in Britain, which in any case was wedded to steam traction. It was this backdrop that gave Yerkes the confidence to tackle the problems of London. He was able to bring with him a team of arguably the best electrical engineers in the world: James Russell Chapman,[7] S.B. Fortenbaugh, and Z.E. Knapp, for example. It is also noteworthy that Yerkes was not only an adroit financier, but could master technical details: he demonstrated this before parliamentary committees, a tribunal, and a royal commission. Moreover, he had the ability to select competent subordinates.

Notes

1. F.K. Plous, undated photocopy in Box 262 YER, London Transport Museum.

2. The term 'Robber Baron' was first used by mid-western farmers when complaining to Congress about extortionate rates charged by railroad companies in the 1880s.

3. Stephen Halliday, *Underground to Everywhere*, p.78.

4. W.J. Passingham, The Romance of London's Underground, p.61.

5. The invasion also consisted of the young and the beautiful – the heiresses who married into the British aristocracy – Winston Churchill's mother being the most famous example.

6. This paragraph is based on T.C. Barker and Michael Robbins, *A History of London Transport*, Vol.2, pp15-21.

7. Chapman had been engaged by Yerkes in Chicago in 1894 and within five years had electrified 400 miles of track. An outstanding electrical engineer, he was paid a salary of £4,123 16s 0d p.a. 'free of income tax'. It may have been paid into a bank account in America, and was twice that of Leslie Green, architect, whom Yerkes appointed. The fact that his salary was substantially lower than that of Yerkes (£10,000) and Perks (£4,500) was one of those facts of life that can be explained on the grounds that he was not taking financial risks. In any event lawyers were paid more than engineers.

CHAPTER ONE

WHY LONDON?

'We shall not speedily look upon his like again.'[1]

Charles Tyson Yerkes' career in Chicago lasted from 1880 to 1899, when he was thrown out – the city council refused under extreme pressure and likely violence to give him 100-year franchises. He had controlled, so he claimed, 40 miles of elevated electric railway, 47 miles of cable tramway, and 432 miles of electric tramway. He left with $20 million in cash and his collection of paintings which he hung in his newly built mansion on Fifth Avenue, New York.

Why did he come to London? One can only guess; he left no diary and no autobiography, and there is no other evidence. After departing from Chicago he was at a loose end – he had no project, no challenges, yet he was still mentally energetic. His personal life was chaotic because he was bored with his wife, from whom he was estranged, his sexual predilections having led him into relationships with many other women. He could not afford a second divorce – the scandal would have affected his financial credibility (he had thus far kept his personal life out of the newspapers and his credit remained good). His wife was living in the Fifth Avenue mansion and so he had no home. His new mistress, Emilie Grigsby, who was forty years younger than Yerkes, had been rejected by the upper ranks of New York society and felt herself to be a social outcast. It is likely that she encouraged Yerkes to come to London where she hoped she would have better success – more of this later. Yerkes was undoubtedly over-confident about London and seriously underestimated the legal and technical difficulties, whilst over-estimating the financial rewards.

When and where did he first meet representatives of the projects that were searching for American money – i.e. the Charing Cross to Hampstead tube scheme and the electrification of the District railway? In a nutshell, we do not know because it is not documented. The prime mover was a solicitor and entrepreneuer called Robert William Perks, who had been associated with the promoters of the Charing Cross tube since 1893 and was expert at getting railway bills through Parliament. Much of his experience in this field had been gained as solicitor to the Metropolitan Railway. By 1892 Perks had purchased a substantial shareholding in the District which, in the expectation that somebody would electrify it, should have been a sound long-term investment. It is possible that he may have been trying to promote a post-Watkin merger between the Metropolitan and the District. At any rate Perks had influence with the District Board, and he needed Yerkes as much as Yerkes needed him. We do know that during the 1890s Yerkes visited London every year; there is some evidence that he was in London in 1896 pondering the Charing Cross-Hampstead tube.[2] Whether he met Perks on this occasion is unclear.

The scheme had been authorised in 1892 but it had proved impossible to finance. The search for American money was therefore on, and according to John Franch (based on the Dreiser papers), two venture capitalists called Thomas Reeves and H.H. Montague Smith were in the USA trying to raise money for the Charing Cross-Hampstead tube. They met New York brokers Arthur Housman and Henry C. Davis; the latter arranged for them to meet Yerkes in Chicago in July 1899.[3] At a later date, Yerkes related that he was in London in 1898 to discuss the District railway with Perks. On the other hand, many years afterwards, Perks made a sworn statement to the US Vice Consul General in London (for a deposition in a dispute regarding Yerkes' estate) in which he said that 1900 was the first year he had met Yerkes. None of this is necessarily sinister, but more likely the problems of memory.

Flashback - Philadelphia

'The life of Yerkes is a study in the ingenuities of financial operations'.[4]

Before going further, we need to rewind to the nineteenth century so that the reader can appreciate the hostile reception that awaited Yerkes and Emilie Grigsby in London.

Yerkes was born in Philadelphia on 25 June 1837 to a middle-class Quaker family, though as Stephen Halliday has aptly put it, '. . . his life showed little evidence of his Quaker upbringing'.[5] His ancestors had come from either Wales or Germany (sources differ). His father was a banker. Yerkes was educated at the Central High School in Philadelphia and his first job was as a clerk in the flour and grain commission and forwarding house of James P. Perot and Brother. He was not paid a salary, but his business aptitude won him $50 from his employer at the end of the first year. In 1859, at the age of twenty-two, he married Susanna Gutteridge Gamble (whose family came from Leicestershire); she was some years older than him. They had six children but only two survived, Charles and Elizabeth. This degree of infant mortality must have been appalling for Susanna. But Yerkes was making progress – he opened his own stockbroker's office, and three years later a banking house at 20 South Third Street. He then bought his first shares in a tram company in Philadelphia – the first evidence of his lifelong interest in financing public transport. In 1868, at the age of thirty-one, he moved to 1535 Girard Avenue, Philadelphia. His father was living in the next house but one. It is not known what influence his father had on him, but their relationship was likely to have been harmonious if they chose to live in close proximity. His life was a series of frequent moves to more prestigious neighbourhoods.

Yerkes was now regarded as a solid man in the 'City of Brotherly Love'.[6] But this was not to last. When the American Civil War broke out in April 1861 Yerkes joined a (Union) Home Guard regiment. He does not appear to have been involved in any military action and was honourably discharged before the war ended in April 1865. In that year he opened a new banking and brokerage office and continued to prosper; towards the end of the decade he moved his family to a substantial house in affluent north Philadelphia. This stage of his life is well summed up by Wesley Towner:

> Before he was thirty he had a decorous wife and two children, a fortune that would have satisfied an average man, and a noticeable tendency to wander from the stuffy confines of monogamy.[7]

There will be more about his wandering from 'the stuffy confines of monogamy' later. The great Chicago fire of October 1871, in which 300 people were killed and 10,000 rendered homeless, was a large-scale disaster and a severe blow for Yerkes. Insurance companies defaulted, and the ensuing loss of financial confidence resulted in panic selling of bonds and shares across America. Yerkes was bankrupted, and had been selling city loan certificates in collusion with the City Treasurer, Joseph F. Marcer. He was then indicted, with Marcer, for embezzlement and, much to Yerkes' surprise, both were imprisoned. He was pardoned and released after seven months following petitions to the Governor of Pennsylvania on 27 September 1872. Maybe he knew too much.

Whilst in prison he told a reporter:

> I have made up my mind to keep my mental strength unimpaired, and think my chances for regaining my former position, financially, are as good as they ever were.[8]

He left prison, his $1 million fortune lost, convinced that he had been a scapegoat. He was embittered and resentful for the rest of his life. It is not too far-fetched to suggest that the trauma of prison may have caused a personality change. Although he more than regained his former fortune, from now on he was stigmatised – an outsider. He could have been expected to try something else, but he had not lost his financial touch and invested shrewdly and paid back all his creditors. He exploited and rebuilt his fortune by judiciously buying and selling stocks following the financial collapse of the railroad magnate Jay Cooke in 1873. Yerkes‘ gamble paid off – he borrowed money at low rates and bought up railroad shares cheaply. When the market recovered he had made $1 million. It is at this point that he entered transport history: he bought up streetcar (horse tram) shares in Philadelphia at knock-down prices. He had realised in prison that street transport could be exploited for the quickest profits.[9]

At the same time his marriage was disintegrating. Yerkes divorced Susanna, 'the final act of social degradation'.[10] He could never forgive a woman for growing old. He married Mary Adelaide Moore in 1881, with whom he had been having an affair. Yerkes called her Mara, and she was by all accounts beautiful with red-gold or dark brown hair (the descriptions vary) and 'haunting green' eyes.[11] She was half his age – seventeen. 'The Venus of Philadelphia', as she was called, was besotted with him and she may have secretly visited him in prison. As Towner puts it, '. . . beauty was a necessary part of his existence'.[12] His blemished reputation now contained a divorce, unusual for the time, as well as a prison sentence. Like him his new wife had not been accepted in the upper reaches of Philadelphian society. Both social outcasts, they moved west – to Chicago – at the end of the year.

'The Carpet-Bagging Brigand': Chicago and the Second Fortune

This name has been given to him by the American historian Philip L. Gerber. In the 'Golden Eighties' Chicago was a frontier city where fortunes were won and lost overnight. The boisterous atmosphere is colourfully evoked by Wesley Towner:

> The Chicago rebuilt since the fire was a city of heroic sights and sounds, a strident, moving, changing, lustily magnificent city, not yet grown, in no way disillusioned with its triumphal march on progress. It was the

campsite of a hundred nationalities, of husky workers, virile, sinewy, and roistering. It was a city of builders, railway men, traders, butchers, manufacturers, adventurers. It was a medley of palaces and shanties, a place of tent shows and opera companies, of velvet trailing in the mud.[13]

The economic importance of Chicago can be measured by the fact that thirty railways ran into the city. It was the ideal arena for a carpet-bagging brigand. What attracted Yerkes was not the climate, not the scenery, and not the architecture, but the stupendous corruption of the city council, where the Aldermen awarded franchises if they were bribed; accordingly they have been called 'Boodle' Aldermen. Yerkes was more than happy to oblige because the great attraction for him was the antiquated transport system.[14] His talent for financial skullduggery could be given full reign. His modus operandi was to borrow money, obtain leases, offer dividend guarantees, create subsidiary companies, and finally issue 'watered' or fictitious bonds i.e. bonds for higher amounts than a company was worth. As Sydney Roberts has written, 'His bookkeeping methods and business tactics were so complicated that a clear account of how he captured control of Chicago's street railways can scarcely be made',[15] and Yerkes was 'nothing less than a genius at financial manipulation'.[16] Few Chicagoans could keep up with him. Aldermen and councillors were open to bribes, or boodle, for the award of franchises. Two arch culprits in this political cesspit were 'Bathouse John' Coughlin, and 'Hinky Dink' Kenna (how could one improve on their names?). It was a young and raw city, where, as someone succinctly put it, 'The hunt for dollars, women, and fame is stronger than anywhere else on Earth'.

According to one source, he took over forty-six small companies in outlying areas which were marginal organisations designed to create suburbs. One of his financing techniques was to issue shares to himself in amounts far beyond the value of his lines and then squeeze huge dividends which he deposited in his own bank account. Theodore Dreiser noted, 'Yerkes should be compared to a man playing chess – the complicated kind with fifteen or twenty opponents. All the moves of each table would be clearly in his own mind'.[17]

So Yerkes prospered; he was forty-five years old and in the prime of life, and he built a mansion on opulent Michigan Avenue for his doting wife, and more importantly, his second art collection. He was unstoppable: when he was forty-nine (in 1886) he bought the North Chicago Street Railroad; four years later he owned the West Chicago Street Railroad Company. He converted both from horse cars to cable haulage. Later they were electrified.[18]

American historians are justifiably hard on Yerkes. As already noted Philip Gerber describes him as a 'carpet-bagging brigand'.[19] Monopoly was of the utmost importance to maximise profits; Yerkes used every device at his disposal to ward off competitors and maintain a monopoly in his territories. When Yerkes' tram drivers went on strike in 1888, the public readily sided with them.

Mr John M. Roach, General Manager of Union Traction in Chicago, said loyally of Yerkes, 'He was always kind, courteous, and considerate to his employees.' In which case, one wonders why they went on strike?

One newspaper called him 'Baron Yerkes' and he was known as the 'Baron' from then on (though much earlier they had admiringly called him 'The Magnificent'). Yet, for all this, Yerkes was indifferent to public opinion, and explained, 'Whatever I do, I do not from any sense of duty, but to satisfy myself, and when I have satisfied myself, I know that I have done the best I can.'[20] He did not suffer from sentimental concepts such as the public good, which meant that he did not have to give his passengers a decent service. His trams were badly lit, dirty, unventilated and worn out. The cable cars had serious technical problems, resulting in breakdowns. Insufficient cars were provided, and when even his shareholders asked for the overcrowding to be alleviated, he made one of the statements for which he will always be remembered: 'It is the people who hang to the straps who pay you your big dividends.'[21] Because Yerkes kept his holdings as separate companies, passengers could not transfer from one line to another without paying a further fare, even though the profits went to the same person – Yerkes. In protest, 'Straphanger Leagues' were formed, as well as other groups which tried to organise boycotts. Yerkes complained: 'Whenever anybody wants to throw some mud at me they have always got it ready made.'[22] A bitter distrust between Yerkes and the Chicago press developed. Newspapers attacked Yerkes, alleging that the failures were due to the cut-price system he had put in. He became the 'archetypal venal traction tycoon of the late 19th century.'[23]

If there was any justice in the world, Yerkes should have been in serious trouble during 1895. On one of his line's live trolley wires fell into the street causing forty-six deaths and 336 injuries. Charges and lawsuits were defeated by bribing jurors. Many decent Chicagoans were outraged and this must be one of the most gruesome examples of the venality in the city at this time.

Between 1894 and 1897 Yerkes acquired eight suburban railways. One of his acquisitions was the Lake Street Elevated railroad in 1894, and in the same year he organised the Union Elevated railroad in order to construct the Union Loop – known as the 'Loop' – the solution to the problem of the lack of a terminus in the city centre. Three elevated railways fed on to it: the South Side, the Lake Street, and the Metropolitan West Side, and after much argument it opened in October 1897. This enabled trains to go round the central district and return to the suburbs. One newspaper called the elevated Loop a 'unique' solution, but another called it a major nuisance. Originally steam-hauled (as in New York), the elevated railways were electrified. In May 1900, a fourth line, the North Western, began services to the Loop.

Despite his professed indifference, Yerkes decided to posture as the 'millionaire-philanthropist' and in 1890 he funded an electric fountain in Lincoln Park costing $23,000 which had coloured lights and spurted water 60ft into the air. It was noted that it was necessary to travel on one of his streetcars to see it. On a grander and more permanent scale, in 1892 he paid for a telescope (the world's largest at the time) for the University of Chicago at a cost of $316,000. It was installed at Williams Bay, Wisconsin, and carries his name. Although it inevitably failed as a public relations exercise, it is a permanent memorial to him, though it has been suggested that the real purpose of the telescope was to demonstrate his financial clout – in case there was a demand for more collateral or a call on loans. Further information about the telescope is available at www.astro.uchicago.edu/yerkes. Continuing his campaign of philanthropy, Yerkes also contributed large sums of money to ensure that the 1893 World Exhibition was held in Chicago[24] (a showcase to tell the world that Chicago was now a civilised city), and he served on its committee on Fine Arts. Much of his own collection was included – 'Yerkes knew what a brigand must do to be both feared and loved'.[25]

However, increasing his fortune depended on a long-term transport monopoly that would yield the $100 million he yearned for and enable him to leave Chicago. To this end he required 50- or 100-year franchises (or 'eternal' franchises as they were despairingly called) and this proved to be his nemesis. The crunch came in 1897 when Yerkes launched his campaign to extend his franchises. Mayor Carter Harrison had been elected on 'The streets belong to the people' campaign. For years Yerkes had bribed members of the Chicago City Council and the Illinois State Legislature, but when he tried to use these methods to win the 'eternal' franchises it was the last straw. He even tried to bribe the State Governor, and on the second attempt, and with the aid of his henchmen, got the Allen Bill through the State Legislature, enabling the City Council to extend the franchises. He purchased a newspaper in the hope of influencing public opinion (which became known as the *Daily Yerkes*), but most of the Chicago press was outraged by the Allen Bill. Civic reformers had gained ground and were able to mobilise public opinion, resulting in a series of mass meetings, demonstrations and potentially violent protests, with brass bands and displays of rope – probably symbolic, though 20,000 badges with a gibbet and noose were distributed. The strength of feeling against Yerkes was understandably strong. A commuter wrote in 1895:

How I would enjoy kicking him up hill and down, kicking him around the curves, kicking him through the tunnels, kicking him until he fell, then kicking him until he got up, kicking him in the ribs, kicking him on the shin, kicking him in the stomach, and kicking him in the back . . . I would then like to finish up with one wild kick that would land him in the middle of Lake Michigan.[26]

In such an atmosphere, on 12 December 1898 the crucial vote was held. The franchise extension was defeated by 36 to 27 votes – not a large majority. The public galleries of the City Council Chamber were packed and the spectators are supposed to have cheered for three minutes. Yerkes had distributed prodigious sums of money, over $1 million in total according to most sources, but the 'boodling' aldermen had fallen out over the distribution of this. Later, when addressing the exclusive Sunset Club after these extraordinary events, Yerkes brazenly said, 'I admit that we want a monopoly of the streets of this city . . . when they say there is bribery in the City Council, why not give us the 50 year franschise we ask for and stop the bribery?'[27]

By the following year (1899), Yerkes claimed to have got control, by amalgamations, of 432 miles of electric tramway, 40 miles of elevated electric railway and 47 miles of cable tramway. This was two-thirds of the Chicago system, but the passengers were 'brimming with ingratitude.'[28] He had built the Loop, the La Salle Street tunnel under the Chicago river (the old swing bridge had caused innumerable delays) and replaced forty-eight horse car lines with cable cars. In 1899, 'Embittered but undaunted, Yerkes characteristically moved on to greener pastures' as Robert Forrey says.[29] To newspaper reporters Yerkes said, 'Chicago is a fine place to make money, but New York is the best place to spend it'.[30]

New York was an older city and by American standards more sophisticated. It was definitely more amusing. Yerkes had opened an office on Wall Street, and moved to his new mansion at 864 Fifth Avenue in New York, next to the Astors.[31] His residence there was theoretical because relations with Mara had become severely strained by his wanderings from the confines of monogamy. The house in Chicago was kept but Mara moved to the Fifth Avenue Mansion in 1896. She had always been in love with him and so was understandably bitter about his unceasing infidelities. He must have created sexual envy in other men; Dreiser wrote that he 'admired Yerkes' bold, instinctive disdain for the conventionalities that bind lesser men' and noted that 'Yerkes' influence over young women on sight was tremendous . . . as if his face or his eye were a formula or philosophic abracadabra which cast a spell. One look at times and the bird was snared – transfixed helpless'. The evidence is that this was not exaggeration, though Gerber suggests that Dreiser did exaggerate Yerkes' sex life; after all, Yerkes worked extremely hard with long hours and would not have had the time and energy for the 'orgies' suggested in Dreiser's *The Titan*.

Appearances with Mara were maintained, and they travelled abroad together. But his flaky reputation could not withstand a second divorce; at that time it would have been too much even for the bankers and financiers, and Mara, now becoming a tragic figure, always hoped for a reconciliation. Yerkes now spent much of his time with his mistress Emilie Grigsby, to whom he had handed over a newly built mansion at 660 Park Avenue in 1898, when she was nineteen. Not a bad present but it meant she was no longer a 'respectable' woman. Yerkes, upon whom the gods continued to smile, sold most of his railroad and tramway holdings for $10, $16 or $20 million (depending on which source you read, the last figure being the most likely) to Widener and Elkins (laughably, they didn't read the small print). Four years later, in 1903, the value of the Chicago system (because the franchises were not being extended) was down to $15 million, according to the city engineer, having been valued at $106 million in 1899. Yerkes did not trust the banking system. He took $20 million in cash to New York. His art collection was loaded flat into Pullman coaches with their seats removed. Horse-drawn wagons carted the paintings through the streets of New York to Fifth Avenue. No form of electric traction could do that.

However, at the turn of the century the political and social climate in the USA was changing: intellectuals and reformers were influencing public opinion and questioning the ethics and morality of the robber barons. President McKinley was assassinated in 1901 and Theodore Roosevelt entered the White House and 'waved a big stick'. He strongly disliked the 'giants of trade'.[32] As Benson Brobick has said of Yerkes,

'... virtually an exile within his own country, he cast about for new adventures and new worlds.'[33] The irrepressible predator, with encouragement from Emilie Grigsby, was making plans for London, where he mistakenly thought there were rich pickings.

From Chicago to London

During the latter part of 1900 Yerkes and Perks were closely in touch, and at a meeting in London in November 1900 discussed both the financing of the Charing Cross tube and the electrification of the District. On the face of it, Yerkes, with a sinister reputation as 'a past master in the art of deception' as Michael Robbins has put it,[34] and R.W. Perks seemed to have little in common, and the *Railway Times* poked fun at their collaboration:

> But what puzzles us more than anything else is that Mr Perks, of anti-gambling fame, is acting as solicitor for this notorious gambler. Perhaps Mr Perks does not know.[35]

Perks undoubtedly did know but was unconcerned about the plight of commuters in Chicago; he could not be too choosy. He and others realised that the money for their schemes could not be raised in London (there was disenchantment with railways and better returns to be had on overseas stocks and shares), yet he needed a return on his sizeable investment in the District railway. Yerkes was a desperate means of salvation, and at this time there was plenty of American capital looking for outlets. We know that Perks was shrewd and the acquisition of wealth sat easily with his Methodist Christianity. He and Yerkes were united in one thing – a strong desire to make money.

Ominously, on his way to London, Yerkes revealed that, 'The secret of success in my business is to buy old junk, fix it up a little, and unload it upon other fellows'.[36] In 1900 London was the largest city in the world and the capital of the largest empire in history, yet it's transport system was a shambles: 'shapeless, ill-co-ordinated, and inconvenient' in the more elegant words of Michael Robbins.[37]

As is well documented, horse-drawn buses served the City and West End, connected the main line termini, and ran out into the northern and western suburbs. The trams were also horse-drawn and did not penetrate either the City or the West End, but had extensive systems in the East End and south of the river. There were sixteen railway companies, nine of which were main line operators, and services were run from thirteen different termini. Two companies were steam-worked sub-surface railways which operated the configuration called the 'Inner Circle', which was fed by lines from the suburbs (and part of which carried goods trains). These were the Metropolitan and the District companies which had languished under apathetic management for several years. The latter was ripe for takeover. There were three electric tubes with no connection to the rest of the system. Four tube railways were projected but were in a 'state of suspended animation' because their promoters were unable to raise money and, as Sprague said, were based on the merits of each route 'with little regard to any other.'[38]

Raising Money

Yerkes sent his agents from New York, Arthur Housman and H.C. Davis of the firm of A.A. Housman & Co., on a reconnaisance trip; he followed them in August 1900. The following month he bought £100,000 of shares in the Charing Cross company. As a result the existing Board resigned and Yerkes became Chairman, and Perks a director. One of Yerkes' first decisions was to extend the line to Golders Green – still open country and ideal for development, and a depot with sheds and sidings was needed. Yerkes went over the route with H.C. Davis, Vice Chairman, on a wet day, and there is an urban myth that at Jack Straw's Castle Yerkes became emotional when:

... the sun came out and illuminated the spires and towers of London below. Yerkes asked, 'Where's London?', and on being shown, turned to his companion with the words, 'Davis I'll make this railway.'[39]

Sir Douglas Fox and W.R. Galbraith were appointed as engineers, and a new construction contract was signed. At the same time a bill was presented to Parliament to authorise the extension from Hampstead to Golders Green. Although this bill was opposed (it was feared that the trees on Hampstead Heath would be damaged by the tunnel) it succeeded, as did the bill for an extension from Kentish Town to Highgate. There was a parliamentary bill, also sponsored by Yerkes, to build five miles of electric tramway to bring passengers from Hendon and Finchley to the tube terminus at Golders Green. This failed. At this point, Yerkes confided his hopes to an American journalist, R.D. Blumenfeld, who recorded in his diary:

> Yerkes ... said to me that in spite of the opposition which he meets at every turn he proposes to go through with it. He has secured the backing of some large American financiers to the extent of £30,000,000, and he predicted to me that a generation hence London will be completely transformed; that people will think nothing of living twenty miles or more from town, owing to electrified trains. He also thinks that the horse omnibus is doomed. Twenty years hence, he says, there will be no horse omnibuses in London. Although he is a very shrewd man, I think he is a good deal of a dreamer ... I drove from Westminster with him in his private hansom.[40]

Blumenfeld misheard due to the noise of the traffic, unless Yerkes was talking himself up, because he never raised as much as £30 million.

Yerkes was to spend much time commuting from America to England; there was a new generation of fast and luxurious steamers. After spending Christmas and New Year in America, he came to England on the Teutonic in January 1901.[41] His agents had bought up enough shares to give him control not only of the Charing Cross line, but the Brompton & Piccadilly (eventually the Piccadilly line) as well as the District. He was interviewed by a *Daily Express* reporter, to whom he expansively declared that no block of shares was too small and none too big. Yerkes sadly, but correctly, formed the view that the District had become 'old junk'. *The Times* said in July 1901:

> For some years he [Yerkes] had had his eye on the Metropolitan and Metropolitan District railways. In America they thought that the way the railways were run was somewhat of a disgrace and his idea was to see if he and his friends could not possess sufficient of the stock of the District railway to make it worth while to make the proposed change [i.e. electrification].[42]

This almost seemed like the seal of approval from the British establishment, and *The Times* quoted him again when he gave evidence to the Board of Trade tribunal on electrification in October of that year:

> I have been coming to London for a number of years and the Metropolitan roads have attracted my attention, and I thought of getting an interest in them and in some way changing them to electric power.
>
> . . . The roads had got into a very bad condition . . . the stock was down very much and everything seemed to be going to the bad.[43]

Which, unfortunately, was true. *The Railway Times*, resenting an American stating the obvious, pointed out that the 'same opinion has prevailed much nearer home for many years.'[44]

The Times speculated that the Central London Railway scheme may have aroused his interest: 'Electrification was in the air . . .'.[45] It would have been familiar territory. Yerkes was obviously well aware of the success of the Central London and was amazed at the lethargy of the Metropolitan and the District managements:

Here were a lot of men, who called themselves business men, in charge of railroad property, sitting by and seeing the Central London road being built. When the Central London really opened, and their trade began to fall away, they did not even move then, but sat and looked further, and have continued to do the same ever since.[46]

Yerkes had never lacked confidence, and had certainty in the deep-level tube. As Stephen Inwood says, he 'was prepared to bet other people's money on it in very large amounts',[47] although he did bet his own. His confidence in buying in to the District railway was based on the assumption that electrification would increase revenue. This had been his experience in Chicago but he quickly found that he did not have the commercial freedom in London that he had enjoyed in Chicago.

A Syndicate – The Metropolitan District Electric Traction Company

With electrification of the District, Yerkes confidently expected to increase revenue substantially, as had happened in the USA. He was able to buy £500,000 District ordinary stock at 25 per cent of its nominal value, followed by £450,000 at 35 per cent, and substantial holdings of debenture and preference stock. The Chairman, J.S. Forbes, told a special meeting of the District in June, held at the Westminster Palace Hotel,[48] that the 'American financiers' were 'masters of the situation' and, romantically, were undertaking to convert the railway to a 'galaxy of light.'[49] In fact, Yerkes had wielded control of the District since March 1901 and Forbes was duly ousted, to the general approval of the financial community. From 5 April to 22 May Yerkes was in America raising money, and on his return to England he told reporters that a syndicate was being formed. The Metropolitan District Electric Traction Company (known as the Traction Company) was duly registered on 15 July 1901 with a capital of £1 million. The first meeting was held on that day at the Hotel

Cecil in the Strand. Yerkes was, of course, elected Chairman. His registered address was his New York office at 54 Wall Street, New York. The capital of £1 million was divided into 50,000 £20 shares, and of these only £63,000 were subscribed for in London; the remainder were in the USA. The directors were Walter Abbott, Boston; Patrick Calhoun, New York; C.A. Grenfell of Throgmorton Avenue; and a Mr Griffith of Austin Friars. The secretary was J. Willcox Brown of Baltimore (for further information on the company structure refer to History of London Transport, Vol.II pp67–9). The stated objectives of the company were to electrify the District railway, build the Brompton & Piccadilly Circus tube, and build the Lots Road power station. These were soon expanded to include the Great Northern & Strand and the Charing Cross (November 1901). Yerkes had advanced £135,000 of his own money to the Traction Company and two of the tube lines by November 1901.

The third tube railway, undoubtedly a sitting duck, was the half-completed and bankrupt Baker Street & Waterloo. After negotiations concluded in March 1902, it was acquired by the Traction Company from the liquidators of London & Globe Finance. Not for the first time and not for the last time, Yerkes triumphed over another robber baron.[50]

A Bigger Syndicate – Underground Electric Railways of London

But as the project gathered momentum, more money was needed for the District railway, Lots Road power station, and the four tube lines. Together with a Boston finance company which had the reassuring name of the Old Colony Trust (and which had been assisting Yerkes' acquisition of District shares), a syndicate was formed to deal in shares for a new company to be called Underground Electric Railways of London (UERL – known later as the Underground Group). This company, formed in April 1902, was to have a capital of £5 million, and was to take over all the powers of the Traction Company and future undertakings. Shareholders in the Traction Company were to be recompensed by 100,000 of the new £10 shares in return for their 50,000 £20 shares. Of the £15 then paid up on the latter, £5 was to be returned in cash (£250,000) and the remaining £500,000 was to be used to meet the £5 call on each of the new shares. Yerkes was at pains to emphasise the greater financial appeal of the larger undertaking which would be operated as a transport network, which, he said with his usual optimism, 'cannot but be profitable.'[51]

It appears that after careful scrutiny the international banker, (Sir) Edgar Speyer[52], believed this too (though he must have regretted it later on), and he now emerged as the power behind Yerkes, undertaking to raise £5 million, in the three financial centres of London, New York, and Boston. In return Speyer was to have strict control over the company, including the appointment of directors, solicitors, and consulting engineers. According to *Tramway and Railway World*, London was 'astonished' by Yerkes' formation of a new company. The *Railway Times* rightly called it a 'bold move', which made the 'pottering financial policy of Mr Forbes look more absurd than ever.'[53]

Although Speyer attracted some British investors, the formation of UERL was treated with scepticism in London financial circles; Yerkes had brought with him a reputation for deception. Like the Traction Company, it was what is now called private equity. When (Sir) Harry Haward, Comptroller of the London County Council, gave evidence to the Royal Commission on London Traffic in July 1903, he summed it up succinctly:

> It seems to me the public were invited to take up these shares in a very roundabout sort of way. First of all, the shares were alloted at par to the Underground Company (UERL), they in their turn sell them to Messrs Speyer Brothers at a price which is not mentioned, then the latter firm sell them to the public at par, and Messrs Speyer Brothers get 6 per cent commission – 1 per cent in cash and 5 per cent in shares – and out of that commission which they receive from the Underground Company they have, I suppose, to pay certain commissions to other people.

As far as I know the public only subscribed about half the £2,000,000, and the underwriters were left with the remaining £1,000,000; but of course, as far as Messrs Speyer Brothers are concerned, they would have unloaded the whole £2,000,000, and the underwriters would have the whole £1,000,000 left on their hands.[54]

Haward said that his evidence for this came from two sources in the City. His main concern was that the public were insufficiently protected; the Underground Group was over-capitalised, and because it was not a statutory company authorised by Act of Parliament, there was a lack of what today would be called transparency. The company was really in the hands of Speyer Brothers:

It seems to me it is important to the public . . . whether this thing is a failure or a success. One can conceive of considerable difficulties arising if it is a failure, and if one is to believe what appears in the newspapers, somewhat similar concerns have been a failure in Chicago. [55]

Haward was rightly concerned about the control the Underground Group, which was non-statutory, would have over statutory companies like the District. The whole point of Yerkes' syndicates and holding companies was to raise capital without parliamentary scrutiny. He was employing strategies of obfuscation he had used successfully in Chicago. The Royal Commission accepted an assurance from Yerkes that he would submit for parliamentary scrutiny any schemes for amalgamation – what else could he say and what else could the commissioners do? Statutory authority had given the Traction Company powers to electrify the District railway in 1901, and powers to build the generating station at Lots Road.

Yerkes' Reception in London

In *The Rise of the Nouveaux Riches*, J. Mordant Crook writes about the influx of American millionaires in London in the 1900s. William Waldorf

Astor is quoted as having said 'America is no place for a gentleman'. In its heyday, 1890–1914, the city of London controlled almost half the flow of international capital, and the attraction was that the 'Imperial City' was the world's banker and as such was the financial lifeline between New York, Johannesburg, Frankfurt and Paris. The author clearly regrets the passing of this, but his concern with Yerkes is trifling; he quotes Professor F.M.L. Thompson who has written that the 'social sieve became decidedly coarser from the 1890s onwards'. Crook therefore asks how else can we explain the 'tolerant reception given to Charles Tyson Yerkes, the Chicago tramcar king, who arrived at the turn of the century, hoping to develop the capital's underground railway?'[56] He relates, as is documented elsewhere, that Yerkes installed his current mistress, Emilie Grigsby, in a villa at Maidenhead and in a house off Berkeley Square, but who knew about this? And did not many other rich Englishmen have mistresses?

We do not know what social circles Yerkes mixed in, if he did at all. Indeed, did he have any friends? Tabloid newspapers had to be more careful what they said about the rich. We know that Yerkes adopted military nomenclature and entitled himself 'Colonel', which he hoped would make him acceptable. In the course of business he met what he regarded as opposition, for example parliamentary committees, having expected to have unlimited freedom as he had in Chicago. Yet he was treated as an individual of consequence; he was listened to with respect by parliamentary committees and the Royal Commission on London Traffic. He had letters published in *The Times* and he had international connections. Yerkes was substantial in every sense of the word. He was capable of great charm, which complemented his physical attractiveness, and this was perceived by those who opposed him.

Although it sounds improbable, there was a brief encounter between Yerkes and Canon Barnett (Canon of Westminster Abbey and founder of Toynbee Hall) on a Baltic cruise in 1896, and it was recorded in Henrietta Barnett's book about her husband, which was published in 1918 (he had died five years previously). There is a letter which Canon Barnett wrote to his brother when the ship was in Kronstadt harbour. The relevant part of it as follows:

We like our company and all mingle well . . . there are the usual Americans. One 'first generation man' as he calls himself, is most amusing. He has made a great fortune in three and a half years, and is now educating himself. He is typical of what a Yankee is thought to be . . . [and proposes] . . . to convey all London about in tunnels. [57]

Given that Canon Barnett and his wife were pious and refined people – and moved in the politest society – it is interesting that Yerkes managed to impress them (assuming this is Yerkes). He must have possessed some of the social graces; he probably presented himself here as the plain, untutored man of business. He was amusing and certainly not a bore. In contrast to the other robber barons, Yerkes knew how to relax and enjoy himself. However, a much later entry shows that Mrs Barnett, very much a middle-class socialist, became less enchanted with Yerkes when he told her:

> . . . that the system of underground travelling he anticipated would cause the erection of a station on the western edge of Hampstead Heath . . . The trains would also bring the builder, and it required no imagination to see the rows of ugly villas such as disfigure Willesden and most of the suburbs of London, in the foreground of that far-reaching and far-famed view. Therefore there was nothing else to do but enlarge the Heath. [58]

This undoubtedly sounds like Yerkes and the Northern line, which took from 1903 (when it is assumed the above entry was written) to 1908, and resulted in the Hampstead Garden Suburb scheme. It must be unlikely that the present residents know that they have an American robber baron to thank for their pleasant neighbourhood.

R.D. Blumenfeld made one other entry in his diary about Yerkes:

November 7 1900
James McNeil Whistler was over from Paris today and holding forth as usual. His latest grievance is that Yerkes proposes to put up a gigantic power house in Chelsea for the electrification of the Underground,

and it is to have enormous chimneys towering far into the sky, it will completely ruin the bend of the Thames made famous by Turner. 'They ought to be drawn and quartered' says the author of *The Gentle Art of Making Enemies*.[59]

Whistler ignored the fact that the river bank was no longer a rural idyll; it had been industrialising since the closure of Cremorne Gardens in the 1870s.

When he died, the Chicago *Daily Tribune* said of London's reaction to the robber baron:

Having bought a franchise for $500,000 and begun work on a "tube" the American syndicate found new difficulties. The London public was fearful and jealous of the foreign invaders. Stories of Mr Yerkes' financial operations and methods in Chicago reached England. His way of doing things at tremendous speed took away the breath of the Britons gave birth to new suspicions. They feared, apparently, that their city would fall into the hands of the magician while they slept overnight, and they put many obstacles in his path.[60]

Notes

1. *Tramway & Railway World* (T&RW), 6 January 1906, p.3.

2. Henrietta Barnett, 'Canon Barnett, His Life, Work and Friends' (1921 ed.), 510–11, 704 in *A History of London Transport* by T.C. Barker and Michael Robbins, Vol.II, p.63.

3. John Franch, *Robber Baron,* p.278.

4. *Daily Tribune*, Chicago, 30.12.05, p.3.

5. Stephen Halliday, *Underground to Everywhere*, p.66.

6. Edwin Lefevre, *What Availeth It?*, p.837. Charles Dickens thoroughly disliked Philadelphia during his American travels and toured the prison in which Yerkes was incarcerated.

7. Wesley Towner, *The Elegant Auctioneers*, pp188–9.

8. John Franch, *Charles Tyson Yerkes 1837–1904.* p.2.

9. Robert Forrey, 'Charles Tyson Yerkes: Philadelphia-born Robber Baron', in *Pennsylvania Magazine of History and Biography*, 1975, 99, (2). p.229 suggests that Yerkes may have enjoyed special privileges in prison because of his banking connections. A friend and business partner frequently visited and was probably transacting deals for him.

10. *Elegant Auctioneers*, p.8.

11. *Robber Baron*, p.89.

12. *Elegant Auctioneers*, p.189.

13. op cit, p.193.

14. Ibid.

15. Sydney I. Roberts, 'Portrait of a Robber Baron: Charles T Yerkes', in *Business History Review*, xxxv (3), 1961 p.448.

16. op cit, p.348.

17. Philip L. Gerber, *The Financier Himself: Dreiser and CT Yerkes.* PMLA. 1973 p.115.

18. Horse trams, or horse cars as they were called, were introduced in Philadelphia and Chicago by 1859, eleven years earlier than in London; cable cars were introduced in America in 1873.

19. Gerber, *Dreiser's Financier*, p.356.

20. *Portrait of a Robber Baron*, p.351.

21. Forrey, *Charles Tyson Yerkes*: p.233.

22. *Robber Baron*, p.117.

23. George W. Hilton, *The Cable Car in America,* p.243.

24. It was claimed that this was the first exhibition to have a Ferris wheel.

25. Gerber. *The Financier Himself,* p.115.

26. *Robber Baron*, p.256.

27. Gerber, *Dreiser's Financier*, p.363.

28. *Elegant Auctioneers*, p.198.

29. Forrey, *Charles Tyson Yerkes*: p.237.

30. op cit, p.236.

31. There is disagreement about the street number; the one quoted here is from Gerber in *Dreiser's Financier* (p.218), and Towner also has this (p.199). Barker and Robbins were told that it was at 811, on the corner of 68th Street (see Vol.II, p.380, note 166). In any event it was on 'Millionaires Row', Yerkes being a neighbour of the Astors, and was facing Central Park. The *New York Times* of 7 April 1910, p.1, gave the number as 564. According to Gerber, it had been completed by 1896, on a site priced at $300,000.

32. Matthew Josephson, *The Robber Barons*, p.337.

33. Benson Bobrick, Labyrinths of Iron. *A History of the World's Subways,* p.129.

34. *History of London Transport*, vol II, p.72.

35. 27 October 1900, p.471.

36. *Portrait of a Robber Baron*, p.371.

37. Michael Robbins, mss B262 in the London Transport Museum.

38. Robbins, op cit, p.4.

39. Desmond F. Croome and Alan A. Jackson, *Rails Through The Clay*, p.45. According to T &RW, he is also reputed to have said from a height overlooking London: 'I would rather have London than the Witwatersrand: there is no gold mine that can compare with London in value', (6 January 1906, p.4). Another urban myth?

40. R.D. Blumenfeld, RDB's Diary, 1930, p.77. quote in *History of London Transport*, Vol.II, p.63 and p.64. Blumenfeld was the London

Correspondent of the New York *Herald Tribune* and editor of the London *Daily Express*.

41. Yerkes commuted across the Atlantic; this was helped by the new generation of ocean liners. *The Teutonic* dated from 1889, and was joined by the *Kaiser Wilhelm Der Grosse*, 1897; *Saxonia*, 1900; *Deutschland*, 1900; and *Carpathia*, 1903, amongst others.

42. 27 July, p.11.

43. 31 October, p.12.

44. 6 July 1901, p.13. Yerkes was not the only American with a desire to modernise and electrify London's public transport. Frank Sprague, the inventor of the multiple-unit system of electric traction (introduced in American cities and on the Paris-Versailles line), was an advocate of electrified rapid-transit systems. In *Engineering Magazine* of October 1901 he rightly argued that London should have a unified management, flat fares, abolition of classes in carriages, and he proposed new routes. The criticisms are not confined to Americans. A temperate and succinct description of the state of the sub-surface railways in London at the turn of the century is to be found in D.N. Dunlop's 'The World's Progress in Electric Traction', in the *Railway Magazine*, January 1902, p.117:

[The lines were] . . . a wonderful piece of engineering work, which other nations were not slow to emulate and improve upon, while London, with characteristic lethargy, rested on her laurels almost to the present day. The Metropolitan and District railways have fallen on evil days . . . They cling to conservative and obsolete methods, and have failed to adapt themselves to modern needs. The accommodation they provide is poor, the surroundings to put it mildly, unattractive. The Metropolitan, in short, spells grime, smoke, heat, and general discomfort.'

And R.D. Blumenfeld recorded in his diary:

I was nearly suffocated today in an Inner Circle steam train between Sloane Square and Temple. The carriage was filled with sulphurous smoke and my fellow-passengers in the packed compartment coughed incessantly. Some day the electrification plans of this stuffy line may be completed, but in the meantime the smoke nuisance is most trying, [p.114].

And to leave no doubt, the *Railway Times* said in September 1899: 'The District railway, over a great portion of the line has become almost intolerable. Some of the stations have long been an anomaly in our civilisation; yet, though electric railway traction has been in commercial use for some fifteen years, nothing practical has yet been done towards introducing it here.' (16 September 1899, p.381).

45. 27 July, p.11.

46. D.N. Dunlop 'The World's Progress in Electric Traction', in *Railway Magazine*, January 1902, p.117.

47. Stephen Inwood, *History of London*, p. 564.

48. The Westminster Palace at the junction of Victoria Street and Tothill Street was built in 1859 and achieved two 'firsts' for the early generation of big hotels; it was not owned by a railway company, and it had lifts. It had thirteen sitting rooms and 130 bedrooms. By the turn of the century it had been superseded by a later generation of hotels and may well have become shabby and out-of-date. It is now Abbey House. Yerkes stayed at the Hotel Cecil which was an opulent and luxurious establishment in the Strand. It had opened in 1886 with 800 rooms and was the largest hotel in Europe. It was demolished in the 1930s, superseded by the Savoy, and replaced by Shell-Mex House, opposite the present Vaudeville Theatre.

49. T&RW, 1901, p.324.

50. The London & Globe was the creation of James Whitaker Wright (1845–1904) who made money in the Australian gold boom but ended up bankrupt. After being sentenced to seven years for fraud he committed suicide. His collapse brought down thirteen stockbrokers in one day.

51. *History of London Transport*, Vol.II, p.71.

52. The House of Speyer had considerable experience in financing American railways. There is information about the controversial figure of Sir Edgar Speyer in *History of London Transport*, Vol.II, p.71, footnote. In David Kynaston's *The City of London*, p.352, he is described as a cultured man who organised promenade concerts at the Queens Hall. He co-founded the Whitechapel Art Gallery. However, he was a prickly character who 'rubbed people . . . the wrong way . . .', but as one of

London's benefactors he 'deserves to be remembered more fondly than he is', (Ibid). He was born of German parentage in New York in 1862 and acquired British nationality. He had been in business in London since 1887 where he was senior partner, and was also a partner in the New York and Frankfurt firms. He gave evidence to the Royal Commission on London Traffic 1905, which is to be found in volume II Qq 6881-6885, and 24604-24775; he submitted written evidence which is in vol III, Appendix 81. Most of this is concerned with responding to allegations made to the Royal Commission by Sir Harry Haward of the London County Council on the financing of UERL. Speyer built a Franco-Florentine palazzo at 46 Grosvenor Street in 1910–11, which ostentatiously had a silver bath. J. Mordant Crook, in *The Rise of the Nouveaux Riches*, p.155, is hostile to Speyer saying that he is 'surely the sinister villain in John Buchan's *Thirty-Nine Steps*.' Unlikely.

53. 1902, p.373.
54. Qq 6700, Vol.ii, p.249.
55. Qq 6710, Vol.ii, p.250.
56. J. Mordant Crook. *The Rise of the Nouveaux Riches*, p.163.
57. quote in *History of London Transport*, Vol.II, p.63.
58. Canon Barnett, *His Life, Work and Friends*, p.312.
59. op cit, p.132.
60. 30 December 1905, p.3.

CHAPTER TWO

YERKES VERSUS THE METROPOLITAN

'Yerkes' Jekyll–Hyde personality lent him dimensions beyond the ordinary financier'.[1]

Why were railway managements in Britain reluctant to electrify their systems in the last twenty years of the nineteenth century? Firstly, there was a historical attachment to steam which had been the basis of the Industrial Revolution and British economic growth – British 'greatness'. Secondly, electricity was regarded as a scientific phenomena – an 'interesting manifestation of an unknown force',[2] its main practical application being telegraphy with an erroneous view that it could not be employed in a mechanical form. This had arisen because science and industry had never had close links. As a result British engineering firms were surprised by the influence of electrical engineering in Germany and America (reasons for the American lead were given in the Introduction). Thirdly, there was also British conservatism and resistance to change. In any event, electric motors were not powerful enough in the 1880s to displace steam locomotives for heavy duty work. Experimental and innovative projects were carried out in France, Germany, Italy, USA, not to mention Hungary, as we shall see shortly.[3]

Nonetheless, the Liverpool Overhead Railway of 1893 was a success. The directors embarked on electrification because steam traction was likely to be hazardous on an elevated railway. A third rail system at 500v dc. was selected. There were twenty-one stations and the line was seven miles long, providing rapid urban transit.[4] In London, two tube railways were opened before the end of the century: the City & South London of 1890 (the first electric underground railway in the world) and the Waterloo & City of 1898. Both these lines were short and commercially disappointing. The two principal sub-surface railways, the Metropolitan and the District, still using steam locomotion, were losing revenue in the 1890s because of atmospheric pollution in the tunnels, passengers having found better ways to travel. Both companies had obtained parliamentary authorisation to electrify their systems, but as already mentioned they could not raise the required capital. A comparable heavy-duty system, the Mersey Railway from Liverpool to Birkenhead, 4¾ miles long, was converted to electricity in 1903 by the Westinghouse Company at its own expense, in order to demonstrate the efficiency of electric traction. In this it succeeded, but was not as remunerative as hoped.

Yerkes was fully acquainted with these problems, having inspected the District and the Inner Circle in 1898. Having got control of the District he was now being thwarted over electrification by an important technicality: the voltage and type of current and its method of collection by trains. It was unthinkable that two systems could be operated on the Inner Circle, and so a rancorous dispute ensued, symptomatic of the traditional antipathy of the two companies – and the way they had been managed.

The Argument

'Mr Yerkes is generally considered a very able man, and one of the greatest authorities on electric traction in great cities . . .'[5]

The District and the Metropolitan, before Yerkes materialised, co-operated sufficiently to orchestrate trials of an electric service between High Street Kensington and Earl's Court, considered suitable because there were sharp curves and gradients – a microcosm of the Inner Circle. The Metropolitan, unwilling to trust the District, also held their own trials privately at their Neasden works. It should be explained that the Metropolitan was able to raise capital for electrification because it had been paying dividends, albeit modest, unlike the District which had not paid a dividend on its ordinary shares since 1882.[6]

The public trials (passengers paid one shilling for the journey) were considered successful, using a low voltage direct-current system with conductor rails.[7] Reports were filed in April, July, and August, culminating in the joint committee (Forbes, Sir Charles Dalrymple and Major Isaacs) and preliminary tenders were invited. Nine were received, including one from the Hungarian company developing the Ganz system. This aroused the interest of the electrical engineers who had supervised the trials, Sir William Preece and Thomas Parker (who had advised on the Liverpool Overhead), and so in January 1901 they visited Budapest to investigate. This system employed alternating current at high voltage transmitted by overhead wires. Manned substations were not required and new carriages were not necessary. The attraction was that it was cheaper, but the disadvantage was that it had never been tested under commercial conditions, and especially in a tunnel. Nonetheless, on 7 February 1901 Preece and Parker decided to recommend it to the two Boards for the Inner Circle.

In early March 1901 both Boards accepted this. Later in the month the situation changed: Preece, for the District, told an astonished Parker at a meeting that the District would not accept the Ganz system. Yerkes now had a controlling interest in the District and had been reminded by his American engineers that direct current systems with low voltage were being used successfully in the USA. This was Yerkes' experience in Chicago, and he probably assumed that direct current conductor rail systems would be installed in London. He must have been dismayed to find otherwise. Yerkes must have been viscerally angry but one of his strengths was his self-control. He had a reputation for never raising his voice. This was a major crisis, and of course he was unimpressed with Preece, who was sacked.

Yerkes was in America from December 1900 to January 1901, returning on the 21st of that month, and then in April and May he was back in America raising money with which he set up the Traction Company. To the Parliamentary Committee taking evidence for the 1901 District Bill, Yerkes made one of his quotable statements: that he would not put a dollar in the Ganz system. This he repeated to the Arbitration Tribunal. It should be noted that, in this Bill, the District wanted to have a clause defining which system the Metropolitan should use when running over their lines, but this was amended by the committee to provide arbitration. The committee expressed the hope that the two companies would amalgamate 'a consummation which would have been reached long ago if the two undertakings had been controlled by businessmen', as the *Railway Times* forcefully put it.[8] The best way for Yerkes to resolve the electrification dispute was to take over the Metropolitan, and on 11 July 1901 he made them an offer. There had been a tortuous history of attempted amalgamation – the sane thing to do, the last time being in 1897–8 when the Metropolitan had made proposals to the District. Yerkes would have been briefed on all this and he was well aware of the weakened position of the Metropolitan. Their ordinary dividend had sunk from 3½ per cent to 2¼ per cent, due to the Central London tube taking traffic from them. He felt they were also weakened by the quarrel over the method of electrification, and might see these offers as a resolution. Above all, he wanted, reasonably, to unify the system (in the event Londoners had to wait another thirty years for this). He made two proposals, though with a touch of delicacy he called them suggestions, which he hoped would appeal to the monetary instincts of the Metropolitan shareholders. In essence, the first suggestion was:

1. To convert the Metropolitan to electric traction (the Inner Circle, the line from Baker Street to Harrow, the City line to Aldgate East, and a share in electrifying the South Western line from Hammersmith to Richmond, which the Traction Company would have to electrify anyway).

2. To provide the electric current, from Lots Road power station.

3. The Traction Company to receive ¾d for each passenger.

Under this arrangement the Metropolitan would bear the operating costs, but the Traction Company would build substations and provide the rolling stock.

If this was not acceptable, his second suggestion was:

1. The Traction Company to work or lease the Metropolitan (bearing operating costs).
2. The Traction Company to pay debentures and fixed charges and a dividend of 3½ per cent on the ordinary shares.
3. To convert the system to electric traction.
4. The Traction Company to receive all revenue.

Both proposals included the offer of seats on the Traction Company Board for the Chairman and one director of the Metropolitan.

Yerkes stated that these offers were open until 3 p.m. on 25 July 1901. This was fourteen days – they were being 'railroaded' with insufficient time in which to consult the shareholders. They did not and the Board turned down the offer. The *Railway Times* resented Yerkes and said:

> . . . most people will recognise that the Metropolitan Board are quite justified in their present attitude to Mr Yerkes and the system to be adopted. The spectacle of the District Board and shareholders being dragged along in the dust by Mr Yerkes is not a dignified one, and we can well understand the reluctance of the Metropolitan company to join in the display. The administration of the Metropolitan Railway in recent years has been bad enough in all conscience, but happily it has not yet sunk to the District level.[9]

The *Railway Times* favoured the Ganz system, and in this, as in other matters, was often wrong.

A prominent shareholder, Albert Kitching (who was Chairman of the Metropolitan's Surplus Lands Committee and a member of the Stock Exchange), was initially in favour of the second proposal. He formed a committee of shareholders which persuaded the Board to strengthen itself by electing himself and Sir William Birt, a railwayman, the ex-General Manager of the Great Eastern. But Kitching subsequently changed his mind and took the view that Yerkes would either make a handsome profit, or the 3½ per cent on the ordinaries would not be paid (Yerkes continually overestimated the profitability of these lines). On the other hand, the travelling public of London would, of course, have got a better service with amalgamation.

An anonymous (and sycophantic) historian of the Metropolitan was contemptuous of Yerkes' technical abilities, and wrote haughtily, 'CT Yerkes personal knowledge of operative electricity was probably of the vicarious order . . . [his] . . . predominance arose from his abilities as a dextrous financier.'[10] Why didn't Yerkes launch a hostile takeover bid? Presumably it would have needed too much money to buy out the Metropolitan shareholders, who clung to their venerable investments.

Given the traditional antagonism between these companies (which did no favours to the people of London), it came as no surprise that the Metropolitan Board turned the offers down flat in July 1901, and their views were expressed publicly at their half-yearly meeting on 26 July 1901. Neither the District nor the newly formed Traction Company were considered financially sound enough to be able to absorb the Metropolitan.

In his frustration, Yerkes wrote to *The Times* in order to give the dispute the oxygen of publicity. His letters can be relished because they are his own words (pardonably embellished by his secretary) and one of the few examples of his literary abilities, given that he left no diary or autobiography. His letter of 31 July opens with a characteristic broadside:

Sir,- It has not been my intention to enter into any public controversy in regard to the electrification of the Metropolitan Railway and the Metropolitan District railway for several reasons, mainly because, so far as I can see, the Metropolitan Company has in years past not improved the position of its stockholders by the controversies in which it has engaged.

So much for Edward Watkin, who is loftily consigned to the dustbin of history. But Yerkes emphasised his principal point: the Ganz system was untried and untested. He went on to explain:

I told . . . the Metropolitan Railway . . . that if the systems which they seemed to adhere to had been tried on a railway like the Metropolitan for a period of three years and had worked successfully I would most willingly adopt it on any work that I had to do with. To take a system which has not been thoroughly tested, not for a few but for many months and even years, is a species of business recklessness which I do not wish to try . . . If the manager of the Metropolitan Railway had commenced this experiment years ago when the Central London was begun, I am satisfied they would have lost some time, but they might have corrected their plant so as not to have been in the humiliating position we find them today. They cannot make the excuse that their credit was poor and they were unable to raise money. They have simply waited until the wolf was at their door and long afterwards.

After dealing with other issues from the Metropolitan's reported meeting, Yerkes concluded his letter on a note of exhortation:

The losses to both companies at the present time are very great, and I believe there is nothing that will stop the continuance of these losses but the running of the roads by electricity. Therefore every day means money, and it is for that reason that I am extremely anxious that not a moment should be lost.

For the moment the Metropolitan had no answer. A reply was made two months later, on 27 September, from the company secretary, G.H. Whissell, who alleged that Yerkes was making inaccurate statements to the press. An icy response quickly appeared the following day from Yerkes:

The fact is that when Messrs Ganz and company made their tender many months ago they must certainly have been aware of what they were going to furnish. When the engineers for the joint committee made their report in which the Ganz system was lauded, proclaimed to be everything that was good, most desirable for the companies to use, and is pushed at us so vigorously, it is supposed they knew what they were talking about.

And the letter ended with a short homily:

> Quarrelling over the matter will not build railroads. We want earnest and industrious application. If the Metropolitan Company will only put a little of that into their actions, instead of making assertions, and show by these acts, rather than by their letters, that they are really in earnest, I have no doubt we will accomplish much more than we are doing at the present time.[11]

Although he was opposed to it, Yerkes decided to see the Ganz system for himself in August. Given the season and the beauty of the Italian lakes and Hungary, one likes to think that Emilie Grigsby may have discreetly accompanied him. Probably not, because he took with him his American colleague William Russell Chapman, who was appointed Chief Electrical Engineer of Underground Electric Railways when it was formed in April 1902, Horace Parshall of the Central London Railway, and Philip Dawson of Robert Blackwell & Co., who had equipped 1,000 miles of tramway. Colonel Yorke and Mr Trotter of the Railway Inspectorate also went. The circular test line on Old Buda Island in the Danube had, for some reason, been dismantled, so they visited the Valtellina line at Lake Como. This was not yet open but was considered, oddly, to be of some relevance to the Inner Circle. This visit caused confusion because Otto Blathy, the Managing Director of Ganz, formed the impression that Yerkes was interested in his system. But the tests which were carried out merely reinforced his opposition, and he later observed that he had been on a 'wild-goose chase.'[12] But Preece and Parker were convinced, and reported in August that it was a 'decided step in advance over any other system in use in the United Kingdom or in America . . .'[13]

The Tribunal

Alfred Lyttleton, KC MP, was appointed Chairman; as he explained, the position was novel because Parliament had, for the first time, devolved to the Board of Trade the task of imposing on a railway company a system of working to which the company is opposed. Ostensibly, arbitration would apply to the Inner Circle, but would in fact apply to the whole system of both companies in order to be workable.

The Underground Group nominated H.F. Parshall as their representative. Thomas Parker was nominated by the Metropolitan. But there was more frustration for Yerkes; at a preliminary hearing on 7 September it was decided to adjourn until 29 September because the Metropolitan representatives had not yet got their expert witnesses from Hungary, particularly Mr Blathy.[14] Lyttleton held a preliminary meeting with the company's legal representatives on 12 October to decide on procedure, but the tribunal did not start hearing evidence until a month later, on 29 October. This was more delay which to Yerkes must have been infuriating, but, as always, he was in full control of his emotions – in public at least. Once started, Yerkes demonstrated his mental stamina and in giving evidence showed that, in the words of *The Times*, he was 'accustomed to make himself master of any subject in discussion even to its most intricate details.'[15] He declared that all the lines in the USA with which he had been involved were worked by low voltage direct-current, and effectively there was no other system used on the large lines in America.

The tribunal aroused great interest in electrical engineering circles, and sat for twelve days over three weeks, completing its deliberations on 15 November. Yerkes had brought a team of electrical engineers from the USA, notably S.B. Fortenbaugh (in addition to Chapman). The latter's expert evidence, over two days, must have carried considerable weight. He had twenty-seven years' experience of railways, ten of which had been exclusively on electric railways with Yerkes in Chicago. He told the tribunal that there would be no difficulty in working the Inner Circle on the third or fourth rail direct-current system; indeed, there was no other system which could be relied upon as safe and economical.[16] Yerkes' personal and financial stake was represented by Mr Fletcher Moulton, KC, who in the customary way flattered the Chairman by calling him a 'prudent man of the world'[17], and described the third rail direct-current system as 'the ordinary system, perfectly well-known, thoroughly tested and proved, [with] no doubts or difficulties about it'.[18] Having taken evidence for a total of twelve days. Lyttleton produced his report on 11 December 1901 with commendable speed; it emphasised the contrast between the tried and tested direct current continuous system and the experimental state of the alternating Ganz system. This could not be recommended in opposition to the District railway on the Inner Circle. As the first historian of the District says, 'At this time not a single yard of railway existed anywhere in the world operated by a 3000 volt alternating current . . .'[19]

Thus, Yerkes won the war of words and the arbitration, but Alfred Lyttleton, who may well have disliked Yerkes' public criticisms of the Metropolitan Railway in the letters columns of *The Times*, took the opportunity to rebuke Yerkes for suddenly changing District policy in April 1901 and conducting open warfare in *The Times*:

> I think it right to add that the manner in which the District Company conducted the preliminary negotiations which took place between the two companies to determine the system of electrical traction was most embarrassing to the Metropolitan Company, and fully justified that company in clearing the matter up by arbitration.[20]

The Metropolitan directors felt vindicated by this. But the *Railway Magazine*, even though it was anti-Yerkes, said wittily:

> In dealing with a force like electricity it is a distinct advantage to a system to have a past as well as a future.[21]

At the heart of the rancour was the issue of amalgamation. There was also a clash of cultures – aggressive American business methods versus the traditional, more gentlemanly British methods. Although Yerkes generally kept calm, he expressed his frustration by saying:

> ... you are tied up here with your Boards of Trade, your Parliament, and the rest, with the result that the man of initiative, the inventor, or the engineer cannot put forth his best work as he could in a country unfettered by regulation, red-tape, and the like.[22]

He wanted, of course, the freedom that he had been used to in America – the freedom to exploit everybody within range. The last word is with Lyttleton, who said rather elegantly of the Inner Circle line, 'it is of vital moment that a service of precise and imperturbable regularity should be maintained.'[23]

In February 1902 Yerkes made his last effort to control the Metropolitan: he offered to provide electric current from his power station at Lots Road. This was flatly rejected – the Metropolitan had allocated land at Neasden for a power station for which the contract for generating equipment was awarded to British Westinghouse; the company issued stock for £1.25 million to finance electrification. The District also offered the Metropolitan terms for running over the Bow and Whitechapel railway so that they could operate trains through from East London to Kings Cross and Paddington. This was refused by the Metropolitan, who countered with the suggestion that there should be a 'temporary fusion' of the two companies' activities for the sake of operational efficiency. This offer made sense but it was rejected by the District. Such was the state of affairs, when at last they turned to the electrification of their permanent way.

Notes

1. Gerber, *The Financier Himself: Dreiser*, p.115.

2. *History of the Metropolitan Railway*, mss p.348.

3. There were some minor, light-duty, electric railways in Britain: the Giant's Causeway, Portrush and Bushmills Railway, 1883; Volk's Electric Railway, Brighton, 1884; Ryde Pier Tramway, 1886; Bessbrook and Newry Railway, 1885; Manx Electric Railway, 1893; and Blackpool Tramways, 1893. Continental European and American technology was relied on. For more information see Michael C. Duffy, *Electric Railways, 1880–1990*.

4. Adrian Jarvis, *Portrait of The Liverpool Overhead Railway*.

5. Edgar Speyer to Royal Commission on London Traffic, 1905 Q 24759

6. The Metropolitan paid 3¾ per cent in 1898, and 2¼ per cent in 1901; the best performing urban railway was the North London which paid 7per cent throughout the 1890s and 6¼ per cent in 1901, but was not electrified until 1911 when it had been taken over by the London & North Western following a sharp decline in revenue.

7. S.B. Fortenbaugh (USA), Electrical Engineer for the Underground wrote that this was a 'very costly' experiment. He said the final bill for the trials was £22,000, which was an over-run of £2,000. At the time, the District claimed that one reason for the trials was to see if electric and steam trains could be operated concurrently (National Archives, MT/6 1000/3). Significantly, Sir John Wolfe Barry, who had been consulting engineer to the District, retired just after Christmas 1900 'dissatisfied with the course which the District company proposed to take in certain respects.' Would he have got wind of Yerkes buy-out?

8. Arbitration was suggested by counsel for the District, Mr Pember, KC, and opposed by Mr Little, KC, for the Metropolitan. The committee passed the Bill on the basis that if, after two months, agreement had not been reached the Board of Trade would appoint a tribunal.

8. 6 July 1901, p.10.

9. 3 August 1901, p.114.

10. *History of the Metropolitan Railway,* mss, nd, Vol.2, p.358.

11. *The Times*, 28 September 1901, p.6.

12. T&RW, 1901, p.654.

13. op cit, 1901 p.434.

14. Postponement was also caused because Colonel J.J. Mellor, Sir Charles McLaren, T. Parker, and A.C. Ellis of the Metropolitan Railway went to inspect the Ganz system on the Valtellina line in September 1901. The Lugano Tramways and certain mountain systems employed the Ganz system: the Jungfrau, Gorngratt, and Engleberg railways, and the Burgdorf and Thun Railway. There was no system comparable, however, to the Inner Circle.

15. 31 October 1901, p.12. Yerkes again displayed his grasp of detail when he gave evidence to parliamentary committees in support of the Brompton & Piccadilly and Charing Cross tube railways the following year.

16. Chapman had worked for Yerkes in Chicago, and although he was chief engineer for the Underground Group, it was S.B. Fortenbaugh, on secondment from General Electric, who advised Chapman to adopt the fourth rail. This was to eliminate interference with telephone and telegraph cables. Yerkes brought over a brilliant team of engineers from the USA.

17. T&RW, 1901, p.655.

18. op cit, p.657.

19. Alexander Edmonds, *A History of the District Railway*, p.196.

20. T&RW, 1901, p.48. Many must have thought that Yerkes richly deserved a public rebuke for his brash way of conducting business, and Lyttleton was of a kind that he had probably never met before. He was a classic example of the gentleman all-rounder. In addition to the skills which he brought to the settlement of this dispute, he had played cricket for England against Australia, played football for England, and excelled at tennis and rackets. When he died in 1914, at the age of fifty-seven, one of his obituaries said 'no one, perhaps, has ever had a greater all-round genius for ball-games' [Wisden]. The dispute over electrification was not his last contact with the Yerkes group of companies; he subsequently arbitrated on the dispute with British Westinghouse on their

unsuccessful turbo-generators at Lots Road power station, though this had to be settled finally by the House of Lords.

21. January 1902, p.75.

22. T&RW, 6 January 1906, p.3.

23. National Archives, RAIL 1027/132.

CHAPTER THREE

YERKES VERSUS J.P. MORGAN

'You've no idea how complicated life is since the row in the Parliamentary Committee.

And does Mr Yerkes live under the earth always?' we asked.

'Yessir, except when he comes up for air, or to read the Parliamentary Reports.'[1]

John Pierpont Morgan, whose London-based son was a bigger fish than Yerkes, his family having been in the game longer,[2] but when it came to the London Underground, Yerkes outwitted him (and a parliamentary committee). Much of this episode is well documented,[3] so need not be repeated here, but there are some gaps which remain to be filled. The clash came about because Morgan's were promoting a tube which, after some adjustments, ran from Hammersmith to north-east London, parallel to Yerkes' Brompton & Piccadilly Circus, and Great Northern & Strand. Furthermore, London United Tramways opened the first electric tram service in the London area from Hammersmith to Hounslow and to Uxbridge on 10 July 1901. Taken separately, these enterprises were a threat to the Yerkes project and became a serious menace when London United joined forces with Morgan. Ironically, it was Yerkes who inadvertently brought this about.

A slight digression is necessary. London United had been formed in 1894 by a Bristol entrepreneur, Sir George White, and in the hands of a highly competent and charismatic tramway manager called James Clifton

Robinson, it provided an efficient service and paid excellent dividends. It had not been easy. The opposition of local authorities and wealthy residents had to be overcome. By 1902, it was carrying 40 million passengers a year. This was the golden age of electric tramways and all over the country local authorities were building tramways to provide cheap travel from city centres to suburbs. In this context, in 1901 Middlesex County Council proposed to build a tramway from Hounslow to Staines. Naturally London United opposed this but Yerkes saw it as an opportunity because Hounslow, the terminus of the District railway, was already his territory.

White was alarmed at Yerkes erupting onto the scene and throwing his weight about. The scheme did not require an Act of Parliament, but authorisation from the Light Railway Commission. At the formal proceedings, Yerkes astonished both proposers and opposers by offering to take the scheme over. He was questioned by Lord Robert Cecil, counsel for Middlesex County Council; part of this interchange is worth quoting:

> Cecil: What is your opinion of the value of these lines from the point of view of the District railway?
>
> Yerkes: They are very valuable to the District railway.
>
> Cecil: And that being so, are you prepared financially to assist with the making of those lines?
>
> Yerkes: Yes.
>
> Cecil: And are you prepared (of course I do not wish to tie you down to details at all) to consider the advisability of taking a lease of those lines?
>
> Yerkes: Yes.
>
> Cecil: And to equip them?
>
> Yerkes: To equip them and operate them.
>
> Cecil: Do you anticipate that there will be any difficulty in finding the capital necessary for that purpose?
>
> Yerkes: None at all; in fact we have it already.

The questions from Mr Lewis Coward for London United Tramways illustrated the hostility to Yerkes. Coward attempted, unsuccessfully, to elicit from him how much capital he had raised:

> Coward: You are prepared to assist these lines financially, you say?
> Yerkes: Yes.
> Coward: To what extent?
> Yerkes: To whatever extent is necessary.
> Coward: That is not an answer to my question. To what extent are you prepared financially to assist? Will you please be a little more definite: do you mean the amount?
> Yerkes: Yes, I do. When I say it is anything that is necessary I mean that it is any amount of money that is required to build the line.
> Coward: Has any amount of money been mentioned yet in connection with it all?

Here the President of the Commission, Lord Jersey, intervened to rule that Yerkes should not be asked to reveal the exact amount. Coward resumed to ask if 'any' amount had been quoted:

> Yerkes: On looking over the lines I think I can guess at what it will cost.
> Coward: When did you look over the lines?
> Yerkes: Yesterday.[4]

In giving these answers Yerkes must have impressed those present with his brisk efficiency. His own staff, about which we know really very little, must have speedily assembled local expertise in order to calculate the cost of land and equipment, and one wonders if his own estimate was similar to that of the Middlesex County Council. Had it been authorised, this tramway would have brought passengers on to the District line at Hounslow, en route for central London (an option which would have worked out faster than taking the tramway to Hammersmith).

To return to the narrative, Sir George White was greatly perturbed by this turn of events. His problem was that Parliament, at that time, would not allow tramlines into central London. He reassessed his company's position in the light of the American presence and decided that his best interests would be to join one of the enemies – J.P. Morgan – where he was welcomed. Their tube line would carry his tramway passengers from Hammersmith to central London and the city. A joint operating company was therefore set up – called London United Electric Railways.

However, the partnership did not work because Morgan did not treat White as an equal partner and would not discuss the various proposals he was making. Although London United were putting less than half the money up (£300,600 against £700,600), they felt that they should have half the control of the project because of the value of the traffic they would bring from their tramway system. Specifically, White wanted an equal interest in the Hammersmith to Charing Cross section.

White was used to being in control and resented the Morgan attitude. He was unable to get them to reply to various letters and the like, and after a few exasperating months decided to withdraw saying 'we have determined that nothing on earth would induce us to continue business relations with that firm'.[5] In fact he had had enough of the tramway business altogether and decided to sell his controlling interest in London United and started negotiations with various possible buyers.

The separation from Morgan's was acrimonious and it is quite probable that White's dislike of the House of Morgan had reached the point where he was happy to scupper their plans by selling out to Speyer and Yerkes. The Morgan group certainly accused White of breaking faith. In any event, Sir George White made a substantial sum and was freed from the 'time consuming and debilitating wranglings in which London United seemed to be permanently embroiled'.[6] Yerkes withdrew London United Electric Railways from the Morgan scheme and their parliamentary Bill fell on a technicality. The rules did not allow a major amendment at this stage, so this was the end of the Morgan tube schemes.

Later, when the dust had settled to some extent, Edgar Speyer was able to give his side of the story when he explained dispassionately to the Royal Commission on London Traffic in 1904 that the

'...transaction was a very simple one...The majority of the Tramway Company's shares were offered to us one morning...This was done without our initiative in any way; we were taken absolutely by surprise... [and]... we naturally availed ourselves of the opportunity of acquiring this control...'[7]

Now, although Speyer came unstuck later in the First World War because of his German ancestry, at this point (1904) he was a respected international banker who would not have been trying to deceive the Royal Commission. He was given a baronetcy two years later. Given that Speyer controlled the Underground Company – the price of the finance provided was a majority of directors on the Board – he would have taken the decision to buy out London United Tramways. He arranged a technical report on the system. The joint company, London United Electric Railways, was now controlled by him and Yerkes.

In the light of all this, it is not altogether clear why Yerkes received so much vitriol, probably because White was a pillar of the British business community and Yerkes was an outsider with a dubious reputation. White did not get off scot-free – he received some criticism in the House of Commons from T.G. Ashton, who had sat on the joint select committee hearing the Morgan Bill, and Ashton tried to get it recommitted. He was unsuccessful and was overruled by the Speaker.

Of course, the House of Morgan was no stranger to ruthless business strategies, and the *Railway Times*, which reported the whole episode at length, commented that Morgan's had been beaten at their own game. There was an aversion to American business methods and the *Railway Times* said, 'We have constantly argued that the exploitation of London transit facilities by American financiers augured well for nobody but themselves.'[8] But who else was going to finance London's underground railways? Whose fault was it if Americans filled this vacuum?

Overall, it was beginning to look as though London's railed transport was being carved up by American robber barons. This caused anxiety in Government and transport circles and was one of the factors that led to the appointment of a royal commission. The *Railway Times* regarded this as procrastination and argued that the London County Council should build tubes 'in the interests of the Metropolitan public'.[9]

Nevertheless, Yerkes' victory did not benefit Londoners. In the view of the historians of London transport, the defeat of the Morgan scheme prevented Londoners from enjoying a useful addition to their transport infrastructure:

> It would have cut travelling time very considerably, particularly on the section between Piccadilly, Fleet Street, and the City and out through Tottenham to Southgate. In the event Southgate was not connected with the underground system until the tube was extended northwards from Finsbury Park in the early 1930s and Tottenham not until the opening of the Victoria line at the end of the 1960s . . . Assuming that both schemes would have gone on and been pressed to a successful conclusion, this was the cost to the London travelling public of Yerkes' victory in 1902.[10]

Triumphant, Yerkes was appointed Chairman of London United Tramways.[11] He assumed his responsibilities in March 1903 (the intervening period had been spent in the USA raising money) and found that his new acquisition was unquestionably providing a far better service in comfort and reliability than had been provided by his Chicago companies. As already noted, Speyer had requested Yerkes' chief electrical engineer, Chapman, produce a technical report on London United Tramways, which confirmed that the line had been built to a high standard and maintained accordingly. Chapman's only concern was that revenue per passenger was less than that on the systems in New York and Boston – not really a valid comparison because these were city centre operations whereas London United was wholly suburban, but with good prospects for revenue growth.

Yerkes concerned himself with financial matters and the highly capable James Clifton Robinson ran the company. A major improvement, the Fulwell Loop, was opened taking in Kingston Bridge and

Hampton Court. We have a report of Yerkes' speech made at the opening ceremony[12] (he must have made many but this serves as an example). Firstly, he reminded his shareholders that London United now had 30 route miles of tramway (much of it was double track) with a capacity for 500,000 passengers a day. He then took the opportunity to dilate on one of his favourite themes, namely the state of public transport in London which was 'particularly behind in transportation service ... [having] never been in a city so backward in this respect'. It was only to be expected, because 'during the last 50 years the English people had not built a single tramway trunk line'. His vision was that his new company, Underground Electric Railways of London, would remedy this, with 'the London United a sort of topping off of their ventures'. With the District railway, he pointed out, it formed a continuous line from Hampton, Hounslow and Southall to the City.

This was undoubtedly true. From west London to north-east London, via the West End, the recently amalgamated Great Northern, Piccadilly & Brompton tube would extend travelling opportunities even further. Yerkes was ahead of his time and advocated flat-rate fares for London (a touch of hypocrisy here – they had been introduced in some American cities though he never introduced flat fares in Chicago; passengers had to buy tickets when changing from one line to another, which enriched him). It took nearly another century to achieve this. This was all part of his vision of creating suburbs from which people would commute to the centre by electric traction.

Yerkes went on to boast that his lines were going in all directions, except south, and he hoped that 'they would join these [southern] suburban districts to the Channel'. It's not clear what he meant and his geography of England was shaky anyway. He reminded his audience (as he often did) that he had a 'great deal of experience of tramway matters, extending over 40 years'. He was full of praise for London United, saying that the only fault with it was that it was 'too good'. He had to clarify this – it was not 'too good for the people who rode, but too good commercially'.

Yerkes was stoutly supported by Speyer, who spoke next and proposed the health of Yerkes and James Clifton Robinson. He then launched into an attack on those who had criticised his raising capital in America and, putting it fairly strongly, said, 'one would suppose that a criminal attempt was being made to throttle London and do its citizens serious injury'. ModerniSation, he said, should have been carried out twenty years ago (as indeed it should), and he concluded somewhat quaintly, 'Had an English Yerkes existed there would have been no need for the American Yerkes to appear on the scene', which could be taken as another indictment of Edward Watkin and J.S. Forbes. Clifton Robinson indulged in some self-promotion, applauding London United and implying that Yerkes was fortunate to be associated with it, as it had 'few rivals, and no superiors, not even in America . . . '. In fact, Clifton Robinson pointed out that over the past two years the 'astuteness and energy' of their late chairman, Sir George White, had overcome the obstacles which enabled them to open the first electric tramway in London.

Notes

1. *Punch*, 10 December 1902, p.397.

2. John Pierpont Morgan, 1837–1913, was one of the leading investment financiers and bankers in the USA. He was born in the same year as Yerkes but came from a higher level of American society, his father having been a prominent international banker (Yerkes' father was only a local banker). Morgan was therefore a second generation robber baron. He built up the family fortune by specialising in railroad re-organisations, and at the end of the century the House of Morgan was involved in corporations such as United States Steel, General Electric, American Telephone & Telegraph, and the New York, New Haven & Hartford Railroad. They had many British contacts. Like Yerkes, J.P. Morgan was an art collector, and much of his collection, valued at $50 million, was gifted to the Metropolitan Museum of Art in New York. When he died his personal estate was valued at $68 million. He made few speeches but is quoted as saying that 'the requisite of credit is character'. The entry in the Dictionary of American Biography, from which this information is taken, makes no mention of his clash with Yerkes in London in 1902. It was probably one of several conflicts with other robber barons.

3. In, amongst others, *History of London Transport*.

4. National Archives. RAIL 1068/162. Yerkes had not been subjected to legalistic questioning in America and could never accept the British adversarial system; he complained about it when giving evidence to the Royal Commission on London Traffic.

5. *Railway Times* (RT) 8.11.02, p.466.

6. op cit, p.181. See also Sir George White, 'A career in transport, 1874–1916' in *Journal of Transport History*. Vol.9, No.2, September 1988.

7. *Royal Commission on London Traffic*, Vol.II q24763.

8. *RT*, 8 November 1902, p.437.

9. op cit, 1. November 1902, p.437.

10. *History of London Transport*, Vol. II, p.85.

11. From March 1903 to June 1905, when he relinquished the post due to the 'onerous duties devolving upon him in his administration of the

District railway' – in the words of the Minutes. Predictably, his attend-
ance at meetings was intermittent; he was away in November and
December 1903, and was not present at several meetings in 1904. Most
of the leg-work was done by the managing director, the capable James
Clifton Robinson, and his contribution to public transport was recognised by his knighthood in June 1905. He had been the pioneer of
electric trams in London. Yerkes concerned himself with the company's
financial affairs and was the link with Speyers. He professed to having
a high opinion of London United, saying that it had been constructed
to high standards and that the rolling stock had been 'extravagantly'
provided. He may have been recalling his Chicago days. It is not clear
whether the company benefited from his stewardship or not. Yerkes
himself had little doubt that it would – see Appendix 8. A summary
of the difficulties with which the company had had to grapple is in
History of *London Transport*, Vol. II, pp.31-4. In 1902–03, London United
paid 8 per cent on its ordinary shares, but this was before the takeover
by the Underground. Yerkes was given leave of absence on 30 October
1905 (no reason minuted) due to illness. The first Board meeting after
his death (in December 1905) was on 6 February 1906 at which the
'deep regret' of the Board was minuted. [London Metropolitan Archives,
1297/LUT1/1.]

12. T&RW. 1903, p.366. The succeeding four paragraphs are based on this.

CHAPTER FOUR

YERKES GETS RESULTS

The Electrification of the District: Case Study No.1

'Is it not wonderful to see how this old London of ours is being roused up in matters of electric traction?'[1]

The impact of Yerkes on London lasted well beyond the grave. It lasts to the present day – it could reasonably be argued that the third-rail system of electrification of southern England is part of his legacy. When he came to London, it was a city with more than a thousand-year history and was the capital of an empire. By 1900 it had a different business culture to a frontier city like Chicago, but Yerkes adjusted to this. He trod carefully. Nevertheless, his ability to raise money had been due to the perception in financial circles that he was an astute manipulator who knew a great deal about the new technology of electric railways – which he did. On meeting bankers face to face, when his eyes became 'penetrating, searching, cunning . . . so that he was trusted by others against their better judgement',[2] thus he got what he wanted.

Because of his considerable experience, Yerkes had more confidence about electrification than his British contemporaries, with the result that his companies got off the mark quickly. One of the consequences of the American approach was that, contrary to Yerkes' public utterances, he and his engineers did not automatically buy British – the most competitive tender was sought, resulting in an early contract with a German firm. For the District, orders were placed in February 1902 for 3,000 tons of conductor rails from Gewerkschaft Deutsche Kaiser in Germany, to be delivered in January or February of the following year and the price to be £5 4s 0d per ton. They also ordered 25,000 porcelain insulators from Doulton & Co. for delivery before February 1903, at a cost of £2,656. It was estimated that the cost for cables, ducts and other equipment would be £800,000 (£53 million in 1995 values), which was more than the rolling stock. Further contracts were signed for the first stages of the conversion of the permanent way in May 1902; work started on cabling and feeders in July, certainly earlier than on the Metropolitan.

The Underground, in the role of contractor, which was to carry out the electrification on behalf of the District, had originally planned to electrify the Inner Circle only. It was quickly realised that steam and electric, with different speeds and acceleration, would not mix, so they were now faced with the conversion of their complete system. Given the size of the task and the capital involved, Perks had to keep providing reassurance to the District shareholders at the annual and half-yearly meetings. Indeed, throughout the process of conversion, the shareholders of both companies (and the stock market) had to be reassured constantly without being given much detailed information. For example, in November 1902 during the debate on the Morgan affair, Perks told the House of Commons that the District railway would be electrified by January 1904. A rash promise to make.

Evidence of progress can be traced, though not accurately, from company and press reports. For example, in October 1902 the *Middlesex Chronicle* reported that electrification was in progress – referring most probably to the Hounslow line, which the District bought out the following year.[3] In December Perks stated that '. . . active progress is being made' (on the whole system), and in the following month the *Middlesex Chronicle* proclaimed that electrification was 'rapidly progressing'. The District working timetables provide corroborative evidence in referring to trains carrying electrical equipment.

W.R. Chapman declared that 'the power house was really the key to the whole situation', as it was. Both companies negotiated contracts for their power stations in the spring of 1902 – Lots Road by the Thames in Chelsea which was to supply all the UERL companies and Neasden for the Metropolitan. The nodal point in the District system was Earl's Court (Baker Street in the Metropolitan system). Neasden power station was better sited for distribution as it was next to the railway it had to supply. The Underground had to lay cables from Lots Road to Earls Court, for which they obtained Parliamentary authority in 1903.

The first section of permanent way to be completed was away from the complications of the tunnels of the Inner Circle – in the open country – and by the end of 1902 the District's Ealing & South Harrow line was completely electrified. This relatively short line had been laid in 1899 and remained undisturbed. It is now the Piccadilly line from Acton Town to Rayners Lane. It was a good choice for a test-bed. Power was supplied by a temporary generating station on the canal at Alperton, and in March 1903 two trains of seven cars were tested. Both were constructed by Brush Electrical and they differed only in the control systems; one was fitted with a British Thomson-Houston system and one had Westinghouse. On 23 June 1903 the District opened their first electricified service, from Mill Hill Park (Acton Town) to Park Royal, predominantly for the Royal Agricultural Show. The service was extended to South Harrow five days later. This was the first of London's electrified surface railways.

The press was invited to look at the new trains; they were, of course, of American design with seats for forty-eight to fifty-two passengers and a lot of standing room, and *The Times*, traditionalist as ever, wondered whether Londoners would ever take to them. The line was called 'Yerkes' American Railway'. However, passengers did take to them and when the Richmond service opened in 1905 the *Richmond & Twickenham Times* said:

> . . . the cars have elicited nothing but expressions of approval. They are cleaner and better lighted and ventilated and the noisesome

vibration to which we have so long been accustomed is reduced considerably making travelling much more pleasant under the new conditions. [4]

This was just as well, as Richmond residents having long been dissatisfied with their train services.[5] Also, in June 1903 Yerkes reported that the work of conversion elsewhere on the system was progressing and that a large number of the ducts for feeder wires had been laid and preparatory work completed. In August the District Board was told that electrification was proceeding, with 1,000 men hard at work, 600 of whom were laying conductor rails and fitting ducts under station platforms. The work was done at night between 1 a.m. and 5 a.m., which inevitably retarded progress but minimised inconvenience to passengers.[6]

Not for public consumption was another attack by Yerkes on the Metropolitan, in March 1904, in the form of an allegation that they were using inflammable materials in their cars. Perks was instructed to protest not only to the company but to the Board of Trade: '. . . you cannot under any circumstances take the chances of a fire in your tunnel, the result of which would be horrible.'[7] Given Yerkes' callous attitude to the victims of accidents on his Chicago tramways, the Metropolitan staff must have wondered what this pious concern was about, until they heard the rumour that Yerkes had set up a company called 'The Non-flammable Wood Company' near London. In the event they sent him details of their (non-flammable) rolling stock.

An additional complication with the Inner Circle was the conversion of the joint lines from Mansion House to Whitechapel, and it was agreed that this was to be done by the Underground. Current for this section was thereafter supplied by them. The work continued through the winter of 1903–04, and to the following June. During this time Perks gave out various non-committal reports on progress at company meetings, designed to prevent the shareholders from becoming restless. He rashly promised that most of the system would be electrified by 1 January 1905. Much was completed by that time, but the system was not ready for commercial operation. The District, justifiably, blamed their suppliers for delays. Another factor was the widening of the line between West Kensington and Hammersmith to accommodate the Great Northern, Piccadilly and Brompton tube on which work started in 1902. This surfaced between West Kensington and Barons Court.

Equally rashly, Perks told the shareholders that the Hounslow line would be ready in January 1903. This was always unlikely and in the event electrified services did not start until June 1905. There is some evidence suggesting that the London & South Western agreed to electrify (or pay for the conversion of) their Putney Bridge–Wimbledon line, and their Studland Road (Hammersmith)–Richmond line (and build the substations at Wimbledon Park and Kew Gardens). In August 1902 the District had obtained powers to electrify the Hounslow branch and these lines as well. The District contracted Underground to electrify all these lines and also eastern 'joint' lines and LT&SR as far as Barking.[8] They had the equipment and expertise and they were only dealing with short lengths of line, though there is no evidence to indicate exactly when the work was done. Under the agreement between the companies, the substations at Studland Road Junction and Putney Bridge were to be constructed by the Underground.

In the autumn of 1903 the possibility of another dispute arose. The Board of Trade had agreed, in February 1902, that the outside positive conductor rail should be positioned 16in from the nearest running rail, and the Underground had proceeded to lay them in this position in accordance with Chapman's specifications. Over twenty months later, in November 1903, Ellis wrote to the Board asking for clarification. If Ellis had never received official notification of this, the probable cause was the confusion within this Government department. The London & South Western Railway had agreed this for the Richmond and Wimbledon lines but most other railway companies had decided on 19¾in. The Underground became concerned that the Board of Trade might be influenced by this and in December 1903 told them, preposterously, that they had converted as much as 80 per cent of their system to the 16in position. Having delayed on this issue the Metropolitan had no alternative but to accept the fait accompli, as by this time they wanted to get on with laying conductor rails.[9] They had to have uniformity because of the Inner Circle.

According to a contemporary report the conversion work was virtually completed by the end of 1904.[10] A minor delay was caused by a burst sewer at West Kensington in December 1904, necessitating the relaying of track there. The District's maintenance sheds at Mill Hill Park were completed also, and after some correspondence with the Board of Trade over signalling, they were brought into service.

Most of what follows is documented but it is worth relating again. On 20 January 1905 the District held a trial run with an electric train from Mill Hill Park (Acton Town) into central London, but clearances at stations were insufficient and it was aborted. This seems like an extraordinary miscalculation. Some platforms had been lengthened to take the longer trains and on the Inner Circle wooden platforms had been replaced with concrete to reduce fire hazard.

Much further work at the stations had to be done and a further trial could not be attempted for nearly two months, but the problems were rectified and the second trial run was successfully made on 28 March. The Metropolitan did better – eight days earlier, when the lines were clear of normal traffic, they had successfully run an electric train from Baker Street to South Kensington and back. There was another trial run to South Kensington and then back to Aldgate on 21 March (which may have been only one trial of several others that were not reported). As a result there were serious anxieties regarding the start of passenger-carrying electric services on the jointly operated Inner Circle, and in the *Railway Magazine* the editor blamed the District for delays (he was anti-American and hostile to Yerkes' lines, whilst sympathetic to the Metropolitan with it's gentlemanly British ways). Yerkes told the chairman of the Metropolitan in April and June that he would not agree to Inner Circle services until the Ealing to Whitechapel service could be started. On Friday 9 June the Board of Trade Inspector approved the electrified South Acton–Hounslow

Barracks line. This success, however, was muted. Hounslow was out in the country, almost remote, so there was no opening ceremony. From Mill Hill Park there were four electric trains an hour to Hounslow, four an hour to South Harrow, and four steam services an hour to Ealing.

The official opening of electrified services on the Inner Circle was intended for the weekend of 1–2 July. But the Gods were not on the side of the District and the Metropolitan. On the first day, Saturday, an electric train came off the rails at South Acton. An early electric train got to Whitechapel and back, but was then stranded at Earls Court because of flooding between Hammersmith and West Kensington caused by a rainstorm. Had the overhead Ganz system been used there would not have been a problem, but nobody would have wanted to reflect on that. Next, as is well documented, conductor rails were dislodged between Sloane Square and St James's Park.[11] The steam services found themselves sandwiched between immobilised electric trains. The District was blamed for not providing better drainage; the company blamed inadequate sewers. In this they were joined by *The Builder*, which blamed the London County Council's pumping station at Chelsea for failing to clear the drainage conduits.[12] The special press train was cancelled, but electric running was resumed the following day. *Tramway and Railway World*, which never criticised companies and was more favourably disposed to the District than the *Railway Magazine*, said:

> The District Company's new trains are a centre of great interest to travellers on the Underground. Their brilliant red colour and the blaze of their electric lights make a great and pleasing contrast with the grimy old steam trains...[13]

On Tuesday 1 August, following successful trials the previous Sunday, electric services from Whitechapel to Richmond started to run from 6.30 a.m. to midnight at half-hourly intervals. It meant that there was an electrified service from one side of London to the other. The

Metropolitan may have, from early August, run a 'horseshoe' service of electric trains, in addition to steam trains, on the Inner Circle from 7.00 a.m. to midnight from South Kensington to Aldgate via Paddington. According to some sources electric services were introduced gradually from 13 September, reducing the running time round the Inner Circle from seventy minutes to fifty. District services to Wimbledon started on 27 August (they had got as far as Putney Bridge on 23 July, and shortly afterwards a service from High Street Kensington to Putney Bridge was put on) and in the following month (on 22 or 24 September – sources vary) the last steam train ran on the Inner Circle. It was the end of an era.

Better management was needed for the District, and Yerkes head-hunted John Young of Glasgow Corporation Tramways and appointed him general manager in November 1904; Yerkes then took over the chairmanship in February 1905. Perks was not up to the challenges facing the District at the crucial point of launching electrified commercial services and, above all, Yerkes expected the credit for electrification. In public, all was sweetness and light at the half-yearly meeting which was, of course, reported in the *Railway Times*. Yerkes assured the shareholders that he would:

> . . . give the undertaking not only his time, but all the energy he could put in to it. He had come a good many miles to take up the work, and he wished it to be the crowning success of his life. . . He had arrived at a point where, while work was a great pleasure, he did not expect to attempt anything after he had got through this [the electrification of the District].[14]

The conversion of the District (whilst still operating services) and the construction of the tube railways has rightly been described as an 'outstanding technical feat',[15] especially as electric traction was still in its infancy. The problems were not technical, however, but economic: 'All Yerkes' financial wizardry and Speyer's multifarious banking connections had to be exploited to the full to raise the capital needed for the UERL [Underground] Enterprises', as Michael Robbins says.[16] The cost of electrifying the District was £1.7 million (it will be remembered that the Traction Company – set up to do this – had an authorised capital of £1 million). The difficulty of raising money in London caused Yerkes and Speyer to produce what he called profit-sharing secured notes (these were anonymous bearer bonds, and readers interested in more details are recommended to read pages 113–5 in volume II of the *History of London Transport*. The Underground Board minutes can also be scrutinised). This was Yerkes' and Speyer's financial 'wizardry' (about which Harry Haward was so sceptical) for which interest had to be paid, so that there was a desperate need to increase revenue. In other words, the enormous capital cost of electrification demanded a greatly increased number of passengers.

Yerkes' intention was to introduce a flat single-class fare to the District and the three tube lines. This had been done successfully by the Central London. His proposal was to divide the District into 2*d* fare zones and charge 2*d* for end-to-end travel on the tubes. This was astute, given that many passengers would not travel that far, but after several postponements the idea was dropped. He claimed that flat fares were available in New York, but he had not introduced them on his lines in Chicago. Instead, at the end of March 1904, return fares to the city were reduced and as a result traffic grew. Profits, however, were still below the level of the 1890s so that all hopes were now pinned on salvation by electrification. Yerkes proposed to increase the trains on the District main line from eighteen to forty per hour; Perks, ever the optimist, predicted an increase of passengers to 100 million. When the new electrified services started the District experienced an increase from 24.7 million to 27 million, but fell short of Perks' prediction of 100 million.

What of the effects of electrification on District staff? Yerkes met the general secretaries of the Amalgamated Society of Railway Servants and of the Associated Society of Locomotive Engineers & Firemen in October 1904 to discuss the industrial relations problems arising from electrification. The latter had a substantial membership of 160 on the District, and wanted to retain two men in the driving cab. The management of the District hoped to pay drivers (motormen) less than steam drivers. This parsimony succeeded and new men came in at a lower rate, but re-trained steam drivers received 'about the same' – whatever that meant.[17] The working day was to be ten hours long with no enhanced payment for Sunday work. It is not clear, and there may well be no record, of what happened to drivers who were not selected for retraining. It is safe to say that some were offered other work, and some were dismissed.

The greatest irony was that just as Yerkes was about to realise a major achievement he became ill, and for much of the summer of 1905 was an invalid. Perks had to take board meetings in July and August. By the autumn he had made a limited and short-term recovery.

More Achievements for Yerkes

The Completion of the Tubes: Case Study No.2

'Is it true, Mr Yerkes,' we asked, 'that you have made some remarkable archaeological discoveries in the course of your excavations?'

'Certainly,' responded the eminent financier, 'I think of permanently taking up residence in a Roman villa which I have restored, and lighting a set of catacombs on the Brush system.'[18]

This is also well documented so need only be summarised, but the story here should be rounded off. As already noted, the Baker Street & Waterloo Railway of 1893 had been acquired by the Traction Company when about half of the tunnelling was completed. It was extended to the Elephant & Castle in order to interchange with the City & South London tube, and was the first Yerkes tube to open, in March 1906, three months after his death. It was quickly, and forever afterwards, known as the Bakerloo (the *Railway Magazine* complained about this shortening of the name). It was the first north–south line through the centre of London and its success was due to its outstanding management by John Pattinson Thomas (1878–1970), who was later appointed operating manager of the Underground's tube railways.

The Brompton & Piccadilly was authorised in 1897 to run from Piccadilly Circus to South Kensington. It was subsequently extended to Hammersmith and this scheme prevailed over the Morgan line. The Great Northern & Strand was authorised in 1899 to run from Finsbury Park to the Strand (renamed Aldwych and closed in 1994). Both these companies were acquired by the Traction Company in September 1901 and were amalgamated, the Piccadilly being extended east to join the Great Northern & Strand at Holborn. It was now called the Great Northern, Piccadilly & Brompton. Yerkes gave evidence to the select committee which was hearing the Brompton & Piccadilly extensions Bill, and, as always, dealt confidently with a range of questions. At the outset he established his credentials in the usual way, when he confirmed that he had controlled 47 miles of cable tramway, 432 miles of electric tramway and 40 miles of electric elevated railway in Chicago, all of which carried 300 million passengers a year. Nobody even hinted, of course, about his departure from Chicago.[19] He managed to reassure the committee about the safety of confluent junctions (in this case at Holborn – the Board of Trade disliked them) when he described such a junction on the Union Elevated Railroad in Chicago where four lines came into one, and where there had not been an accident for five years.[20] Counsel for the Company, Mr K. Littler, KC, produced an opportunity for Yerkes to expound his gospel:

> Littler: In your great experience you would not have lent your name to this, I suppose, unless you were of [the] opinion that there was an extremely strong case for the system of railways you are now developing.

> Yerkes: There are a number of points in that. I have got to a time when I am not compelled to go into this business, but seeing the way things were in London, I made up my mind this would be my last effort. I know a man is always judged by the last work he does, not the first. He may be successful in 20 efforts and fail in his twenty first, and all he has done goes for nothing; so I am very anxious in all this business to have everything arranged just as well as I can possibly have.[21]

It was opened in December 1906, and was thereafter known as the Piccadilly line.

Yerkes did not like the Parliamentary Committee system – he was used to more freedom and saw them as obstructive. If it was an ordeal then he coped with it pretty well, but he told the Royal Commission on London Traffic, 'I have noticed that witnesses are examined by most astute counsel, and frequently made to say, or seem to say, what they do not really mean, and, in fact, the whole subject is given the appearance of a trial in court.'[22]

The Charing Cross, Euston & Hampstead Railway, the first line in which Yerkes had become interested (and which may have been instrumental in attracting him to London), was the last to be opened, in June 1907. Yerkes, with foresight, had improved the scheme by extending it at both ends; the two northern branches to potential population centres at Golders Green and to Archway Tavern (for Highgate) respectively, and the West End terminus south to Charing Cross where passengers could interchange from the District railway (and the main line station).

These changes meant they had to go back to Parliament, and Yerkes attended the select committee; he was asked by his lordships if the line was likely to be viable and useful to the public. Yerkes confidently asserted: 'In all my calculation I have estimated that we will earn over 4 per cent on the capital we invest.'[23] The committee was concerned about the risk of fire in tunnels and Yerkes gave assurances that non-flammable materials would be used on the track and in the cars. He said that the latter would be constructed with steel and asbestos. The extension northwards under Hampstead Heath was opposed for fear of damaging the Heath and, in the case of Lord Iveagh, for fear of damaging his property (Heath House, adjacent to Jack Straw's castle) by vibration.[24] His counsel, Mr Joseph Shaw, said, 'With regard to the question of damage you know that there is a beautiful uncertainty always about making tubes or tunnels', to which Yerkes quietly replied, 'There is not much uncertainty I think.' In fact, a slight deviation was made and Yerkes patiently explained that vibration was unlikely as they would be using heavier rails – a section of which would be tested first on the District line – and seven car trains with three motors. There would not be the vibration problems which had been experienced on the Central London Railway. Yerkes was listened to with respect and Lord Iveagh did not get much sympathy – it was one of several homes which he owned. It was a case of the British aristocracy siding with an American robber baron for the benefit of Londoners. Under pressure, Yerkes was calm and authoritative, which is why he generally got his own way.

The stations were to the designs of Leslie W. Green (1874–1908). This crucial and highly successful appointment appears to have been made by Yerkes himself; he reported it to the Underground Board on 22 September 1903, explaining that Green was to be responsible for station buildings above ground level for all four railways in the group. There is no record of how and where they met.[25] Leslie Green's address is stated as 71 Strand, close to the Hotel Cecil where Yerkes stayed. It is most unlikely that they would have met in the bar of the hotel, especially as Yerkes did not drink alcohol or smoke. He did not drink tea either. One possibility is that they were introduced by Harry Wharton Ford, the architect to the District. In any event, Yerkes' talent spotting would have been done by agents. The salary of £2,000 was generous for somebody of twenty-nine, and once again Yerkes showed himself to be an astute judge of ability. He interested himself in design and decoration and he and Green instigated an early attempt at corporate identity in the design of stations on the three tube railways. Green was to work alongside Harry Wharton Ford.

Standardisation gave all three Yerkes tubes the same station design with the same lettering, done during 1906–07. The 'UNDERGROUND' format was introduced in 1908. Green's work showed great imagination, and he completed fifty stations in five years. The frontages were of dark red, glazed bricks, and the platform walls had bands of tiles in different colours to help passengers identify stations. The stations formed plinths so that the airspace over them could be let out. Green designed booking halls with art-nouveau grilles and doors on lifts. Green died tragically young at thirty-three, worn out by the pace that Yerkes set according to some sources, but in fact chronically ill with tuberculosis. Stanley Heaps was his assistant and he took over. Yerkes' life was also coming to an end.

As with the District, contracts were awarded on a competitive basis. For example, 108 cars for the Baker Street & Waterloo (B&W) were ordered from the USA, 218 cars for the Great Northern & Piccadilly (the future Piccadilly line) from France and Hungary, but 150 cars for the Charing Cross to Golders Green line (the future Northern line) were mainly of British construction – to the relief of the *Railway Times*. Purchasing abroad was unpopular.

In common with the District the tube lines fell far short of their traffic forecasts. Indeed, a tramway consultant wildly forecast 60 million passengers a year for the Piccadilly, 50 million for the Hampstead and 35 million for the Bakerloo. In the event, the Bakerloo only achieved one third of the predicted passengers. It was neatly put: 'Alas, all these sanguine prophets were soon to be sadly confounded.'[26]

Yerkes' Underground introduced some American safety innovations on the District lines and in the tubes, one of the most important being automatic signalling, using track circuits so that signals defaulted to danger as trains passed and simultaneously raising a trainstop arm which engaged a brake lever on any train which attempted to pass the signal. This was an early form of automatic train protection. Illuminated track diagrams were installed in signal boxes which showed signalmen where the trains were. This was standard throughout the District by 1908, ahead of the Metropolitan which had automatic signalling installed on the northern section of the Inner Circle by mid-1909 and on the tubes from the start.

Consequences

Although American investment capital was flowing into London and the upper classes were being penetrated by a plutocracy of self-made men, Yerkes got, at best, a mixed reception:

> If one could believe half the stories in circulation as to how he obtained concessions from municipalities [in Chicago] it would turn the hair grey in the twinkling of an eye . . . it is certain he has not come over to England to beautify the country or benefit the people at large.[27]

The crunch came at the end of 1905 when Yerkes was back in America and motor bus competition was just beginning to bite. His miscalculations started to surface. Speyer had a major crisis on his hands – he needed a transport specialist for the Underground Group whilst he fulfilled the role of chairman and managed the finances, so he engaged (Sir) George Stegmann Gibb, general manager of the North Eastern Railway from 1891. Gibb was university educated and more sophisticated than the run of railway managers at the time, such as Forbes and Watkin. He had been using new analytical techniques, mainly statistical, in the management of arguably the best railway in the country. Speyer got the man he needed. Gibb was appointed Deputy Chairman and managing director of Underground Electric Railways, and Chairman and managing director of the District railway, from 1 January 1906. This was a heavy workload and near enough the proverbial bed of nails; as Oliver Green says, it was 'a difficult time for both of them, taking over a company which had committed very large sums of money on electrification and new tube construction without, as yet, any worthwhile financial return'.[28] No wonder it has been called 'Sir George Gibb's frightful first year'.[29]

Indeed at the half-yearly meeting of the District Company in February 1906, six months after electrification, it was revealed that expenditure was up by £30,000, with income slightly up by £6,000. There was a loss of £36,000. This was the last meeting at which Perks (as vice-chairman) took a significant part; he resigned the following year. Working losses rose to £40,000 in the first half of 1906 and dropped only slightly to £38,500 in the second half. The total loss, with other payments, was £100,000 and as District shares fell the *Railway Times* thought that the company was 'not far removed from bankruptcy'.[30]

At this point Gibb recruited Frank Pick, who had worked with him on the North Eastern Railway and had used, as a means of measuring efficiency, passenger–mile and ton–mile calculations. Gibb now decided that Yerkes' fare reductions had been too drastic, and from 1 September 1906 he increased return fares so that they were double single fares and abandoned, once and for all, Yerkes' long-term objective of moving towards 2d fare zones.

Gibb advocated closer working amongst the Underground tubes but amalgamation was resisted by the American shareholders, who believed that they could make capital gains by selling shares in the individual companies when profits started to come in.[31] The American institutional investors decided to stave off bankruptcy by appointing Albert Stanley, from the New Jersey tramways, to join the Underground to provide an aggressive management style, and to 'keep an eye on Gibb'.[32] He arrived as general manager in mid-1907, and became a director the following year; he took over from Gibb as managing director in 1910. Stanley reduced wasteful competition. Nevertheless, all London railways were suffering from the effects of high capital expenditure, the competition with buses and insufficient passenger growth. The Metropolitan's dividend fell from 3 per cent to ½ per cent. The companies agreed on a general fare increase; the Central London ceased to be a Twopenny Tube. There were frequency and timetable improvements on 1 January 1907, just before Stanley's arrival.[33] The Underground companies did better than the others in increasing revenue, in contrast to the poor performance of other lines. The District railway improved; revenue grew as services got better but the company still could not pay a dividend on its ordinary shares: '. . . the Underground, ably managed, was steadily moving away from the abyss and up the steep slope to profitability; but it was a hard climb'.[34]

The District and the Metropolitan railways gained slightly from fare increases in July 1907, but by February 1908 bus competition was so relentless that the companies were forced to move to a greater level of co-operation. They agreed on joint publicity and marketing as the U-N-D-E-R-G-R-O-U-N-D (this with white lettering on a light blue background). Through booking was extended and passengers were provided with a standard map of the whole system, and a similar map was displayed on stations. To make the geography clearer the names of two stations were changed: Tottenham Court Road station became Goodge Street and Oxford Street became Tottenham Court Road on the Hampstead line (Northern line). But the financial outlook was still gloomy.

£15 million had been raised by UERL, which required annual interest payments of nearly half a million pounds, and there was the obligation to redeem £7 million of the 'profit sharing' notes by 30 June 1908. For this, the profits had failed to materialise. Yerkes had always been over-optimistic about passenger growth. He had engaged Stephen Sellon, consultant engineer to the British Electric Traction Company, to estimate revenue on the three tubes; like many gurus before and after, Sellon got it completely wrong. He predicted that the Bakerloo would carry 35 million passengers annually (for the first full year it carried 20.6 million), the Hampstead (Northern) would carry 50 million (it carried 25.2), and the Piccadilly 60 million (25.8). The total was 71.6 million against the prediction of 145 million. Perks had also been hopelessly optimistic about the results of electrification on the District (though this was also to keep the shareholders quiet).

Speyer's next move was to try and offload the Underground onto the London County Council, which he hoped would be interested in municipal ownership. This was first broached with the leader of the Progressive Party, T. McKinnon Wood, across the dinner table at the home of the Fabians Sydney and Beatrice Webb in April 1906. It came to nothing. Speyer returned to the issue of state support, more publicly, at the opening of the Charing Cross and Hampstead tube, in June 1907. In his speech, in the presence of David Lloyd George, he reminded his audience and the press that London was the only city where no subsidy or support was given by the state to public transport. He pointed out that there were advantages in running public transport under one authority.[35] As the redemption date for the £100 'profit sharing' notes approached, their value fell to £35 and Speyer had to pay £175,000 from the bank's resources to appease the holders who were now threatening bankruptcy proceedings.

Speyer and Gibb produced a proposal to exchange the notes for a mixture of fixed interest bonds redeemable on 1 January 1933, and preference shares due on 1 January 1948. In the face of liquidation, 96 per cent of the shareholders accepted their scheme, as did the owners of profit sharing notes. They had little choice. By this time the District was starting to make a profit – by 1909 it had an operating surplus of £45,000 which rose to £125,000 in 1910. The three Underground tubes were merged and formed into the London Electric Railway Company in the same year, which yielded savings in administration and an increased profit. Gibb retired in 1910 (probably due to American influence) and Stanley took over and pushed through the proposals which Gibb had made. In 1912 the Underground took over London's biggest bus operator, the London General Omnibus Company (which had regularly paid a dividend of 12 per cent) followed in the same year by Metropolitan Electric Tramways. In the succeeding year (1913), two other principal tube railways were taken over – the Central London (affected by bus competition) and the City & South London (the eastern arm of the Northern line), forming the London Traffic Combine (known as 'The Combine'), and arguably preparing the way for the final amalgamations of 1933.

Notes

1. T&RW, 1901, p.632.
2. London Transport Museum, Box 262 YER.
3. At the knock-down price of £165,714, according to Perks' report to his shareholders. It had cost £330,000 to build.
4. 5 August 1905 p.4.
5. Local papers had been full of complaints, mainly against the London & South Western; see my *Railways of Richmond upon Thames*, 1991.
6. In contrast to the time of writing (2007) where the contractors – Metronet – have closed down the Circle line for entire weekends on several occasions in order to to carry out maintenance, and are now bankrupt.
7. History of the Metropolitan Railway, mss p.362.
8. T &RW, 2 February 1905, p.6.
9. National Archives, MT6 1227/1.
10. T&RW, 9 February 1905, p.141.
11. J.R. Day states in *The Story of London's Underground*, 1972, p.79, that the District track was laid 'less accurately' than that of the Metropolitan. Unfortunately, he cites no evidence for what is a serious criticism of W.E. Hanson, the manager responsible.
12. 8 July 1905, p.37. This pumping station was next to Lots Road power station.
13. 13 July 1905, p.36.
14. 11 February 1905, p.138.
15. *History of London Transport*, Vol.II, p.113.
16. Ibid.
17. *History of London Transport*, Vol.II, p.316.
18. *Punch*, 10 December 1902, p.397.
19. Evidence to select committee on Brompton & Piccadilly Circus Railway (New Lines etc) 29 April 1902. House of Lords Records.
20. It looks as though the Board of Trade had not caught up with automatic signalling, which protected the junctions.
21. Evidence to select committee on Brompton & Piccadilly Circus Railway.

22. Appendix 61 q20152, p.628.

23. Evidence to select committee on Charing Cross, Euston & Hampstead Railway (no. 1) Bill, 1 May 1902. House of Lords Records.

24. Lord Iveagh (of Kenwood House) and Yerkes had something in common – they were both art collectors.

25. Leslie Green was educated at Dover College and studied in Paris for a year. He opened his own practice in 1897.

26. *History of London Transport*, Vol.II, p.116.

27. *RT* 27 October 1900, p.471.

28. Oliver Green, *The London Underground: An Illustrated History*, p.30.

29. *History of London Transport*, Vol.II, p.139.

30. quote in *History of London Transport*, Vol.II, p.140.

31. Halliday, p.79.

32. op cit, p.83.

33. Details of these are in *History of London Transport*, Vol.II, pp146–9.

34. op cit, p.150.

35. *The Times*, 22 June 1907, p.3.

CHAPTER FIVE

YERKES AND HIS WOMEN

The Wives

He was disloyal to both of them.

We know little about his first wife, Susanna Gutteridge Gamble, except that her antecedents came from Leicestershire and she was older than Yerkes. They may have been childhood friends. Of their six children, four died, which must have been appalling for her. This would have taken its toll and she must have aged, with the result that Yerkes grew tired of her – he could never forgive a woman for growing old. He obtained a divorce from Susanna in Fargo, which was the 'final act of social degradation', as Towner describes it,[1] and married Mary Adelaide Moore in 1881. She was born in 1856 and so was twenty-five; he called her Mara. He had been involved with her since she was seventeen and long before he left Susanna, so she took risks with her reputation – there is some evidence that she visited him when in prison. It is probable but not certain that they used a house of assignation in Philadelphia. She was undoubtedly beautiful with red-gold hair (like Emilie Grigsby; see page 13 of picture section).

She was Irish and described as a Celtic beauty, but was considered ostentatious. Someone, probably Yerkes, called her the 'Venus of Philadelphia'. When she met Yerkes she had a craving for affection and fell passionately in love with him. She was not as intelligent as Yerkes and did not provide him with enough mental or intellectual stimulation, but she was equally ambitious. Moreover, her perception was that Yerkes was in a higher social class and that he would be her passport to the upper reaches of Chicago society. But social rules and rigid conventions did not limit Mara and she was never accepted by the social elite she yearned to join. Because of this she subsequently welcomed the move to New York, but she had little success amongst the upper classes there, who were also conservative and snobbish.

Not long after marrying her, Yerkes started to stray from the restrictions of domesticity and although he was as discreet as possible, rumours circulated, and business associates kept him away from their wives and daughters. This curtailed Mara's social life. Yerkes broke all the rules of society – he challenged the one-life one-love ethos at a time when, although many disagreed with it, few actively broke it. He had no spiritual, religious or moral sensitivity and as a result had no conscience – he did not care about the difference between right and wrong, only about the difference between strength and weakness. Mara's big mistake was to grow older and Yerkes must have wished he could divorce her. Appearances were kept up and she resided in the mansion on Fifth Avenue – the problem was that he did not, and in her loneliness she descended into alcoholism. After Yerkes' death things got worse.

On 30 January 1906, only a month after her husband's death, she married a hoaxer, Wilson Mizner. He was younger than her. She was forty-nine and had not lost her looks. The marriage lasted fifteen days and Mizner was prevented from any attempts at looting the mansion by Louis Owseley and the security officers of the Central Trust Company (who were trustees of Yerkes' estate). They searched Mizner every time he left the mansion. Nevertheless, he did get away with some jewellery and Yerkes' electric automobile.

Later, Mara denied that the marriage had taken place. She lingered on in the mansion for four years, then moved to the Plaza Hotel as the art collection and the mansion had to be sold. She died of pneumonia in April 1910, aged fifty-four.

The Kentucky Beauty

'She had gone to the bad, and she had done it magnificently.'[2]

Throughout his life, Yerkes wandered from the stuffy confines of monogamy, as Wesley Towner so delicately puts it, and had many affairs with women:

> There were stenographers and actresses, and young girls being trained for the stage . . . There were girls who wished to play the violin, girls who wished only to wear golden gowns. There were those who yearned for diamond bracelets. . . There were wives of other titans, wives of Bohemians who lived on Yerkes pensions. . . [3]

Of all his mistresses, the most important was Emilie Busbey Grigsby. She played a significant but unacknowledged role in the modernisation of London's underground railways. For reasons that will be described, Emilie encouraged Yerkes to come to London, and then with her social graces and undoubted charm, facilitated introductions and business contacts that smoothed his path towards the British establishment.

After Yerkes' death in 1905, Emilie lived for another fifty-nine years, mostly in London. To some extent she reinvented herself, as is possible in another country, but it seems she never achieved the high social recognition in England that she craved. She was always socially ambiguous, promoting herself as a 'mysterious wealthy American heiress'. In the upper reaches of London society, this didn't work; there was too much mystery – especially for a lady. As far as possible she buried any connection with Yerkes and his financial operations (although the money he had provided lasted her whole life). But her early years were the stuff of scandal.

It seems that she never revealed her date and place of birth. She died in London on 11 February 1964, and her death certificate states her age as 'about 83'. She was born in 1879 in Kentucky. When living in England she claimed that her birthday was on St George's Day, but this may have been a device in pursuit of Englishness – a strategy to gain acceptance and approval – with a renunciation of America. According to Wesley Towner, one of her ancestors was Carter Braxton who had been a signatory to the Declaration of Independence. Her brother was named Braxton in his memory. Her early childhood was uneventful; she was born into a family of some social standing, although her father – Colonel Louis Grigsby – died not long after the birth of her brother and herself. Either extreme poverty, some sort of scandal, or stupidity, reduced her mother to keeping a house of assignation in Cincinnati. Emilie did not know about this at the time; she was sent a long way from home to a convent near New York for her education (at Yerkes' expense). One version of events is that the Mother Superior revealed her mother's profession to Emilie, insisting that she 'reclaim' her. There is a remarkable similarity to George Bernard Shaw's play of the same epoch, *Mrs Warren's Profession*.

Thus Emilie's background was flawed, which would not have mattered if she had not been driven by relentless ambition. We do not know if Yerkes patronised this establishment before it was closed by the police in 1897. If not, how did he get to know the Grigsbys? At any rate he became friendly with the mother and possibly financed Emilie's convent education. If so, why? There is another version, related by the Chicago *Sunday Tribune*, to the effect that mother and daughter were living in a boarding house in New York when Yerkes met them, courted her, and 'prevailed', as they quaintly put it.[4]

Philip Gerber says that it was in 1894, when Yerkes was fifty-seven, that Emilie became a 'fixed idea in his mind.'[5] She would have been fifteen at this time. His mansion at 864 Fifth Avenue was nearing completion, where (if only he would live there) he would enjoy a more than opulent lifestyle; it had a marble staircase, a magnificent conservatory complete with birds, a gold bedstead which had belonged either to the King of the Belgians or mad King Otto of Bavaria (sources vary), and 'two immense art galleries where he hung the paintings gathered in his European travels.'[6] He also had a collection of Sevres porcelain. His office windows were of medieval stained glass. Yerkes was immensely proud of his art collection. He differed from the bigger robber barons such as Rockefeller and Carnegie, who spent little on themselves and lived in relatively modest styles. On the other hand he was a major contributor to the American plundering of British art at this time.

When the brothel in Cincinnati was closed in 1897, mother, daughter and Braxton were installed by Yerkes at the Hotel Grenoble, New York. He employed Braxton as a secretary. Yerkes had given him a sinecure to ensure his discretion – he may not have been overwhelmingly brilliant. Thus, although Yerkes maintained a home and kept up appearances; he was supporting the Grigsby family.

Here they had 'an elaborate suite of rooms, servants of their own, a stable with saddle horses and carriages, for all the needs of women of fashion'.[7] Emilie was on the point of leaving school, and was 'on the way to become [sic] a reigning belle' in 'areas of New York society which granted her tentative acceptance.'[8] Like Thackeray's Becky Sharp a century earlier, Emilie needed to marry in order to attain a position in society. She started presenting herself to the upper levels of New York society as an heiress under the protection of her mother.[9] And so her name was linked from time to time with sons of prominent families in her relentless pursuit of an advantageous marriage.

However, as in *Vanity Fair,* the truth developed a tendency to seep out. A Mrs Spencer Trask of Yaddo, Saratoga, dropped her when she learnt of Emilie's background. Emilie's name was then linked to that of Captain Richmond Pearson Hobson[10] of Old Point Comfort, Virginia, a naval hero of the 1898 Spanish-American War, but she was rejected again. This was in March 1901, not long before she came to England and when Yerkes had gained control of the District railway.

The climax came in the dining room of the Waldorf-Astoria, New York, at a dinner given for her mother by Admiral Sigsbee, another hero of the Cuban War. Sue Grigsby was recognised by a drunken ex-client from Cincinnati. It is difficult to establish exactly when this incident took place as it was covered up at the time and reported by the Chicago *Sunday Tribune* some years later, but it was probably in 1901 or 1902. It was a catastrophe.[11] Yerkes then went to considerable lengths to rescue Emilie's reputation by issuing a statement of denial, posing as 'Captain

Grigsby'. All to no avail. The incident is included in *The Titan*, Dreiser having read the Chicago *Sunday Tribune* and interviewed friends. So it was in life. According to Dreiser it was not until this point that Emilie knew of her mother's profession.

Towner says that, in New York, she was only taken up by matrons in the less fashionable echelons of society who did not bother to check her background. An example was Mrs Dunlap Hopkins (see below).

A further, and possibly final, attempt to get accepted by New York society ended in failure in the summer of 1903. 'Emilie Grigsby Almost A Victor', as the Chicago *Daily Tribune* later put it (just after Yerkes had safely died).[12] In the summer of 1903, Emilie had cultivated a New York society hostess called Mrs James Kernochan in Paris, who had invited her to her home in America. However, a few days later they were driving through the streets of Paris when they passed a barrow loaded with strawberries. Emilie impulsively and ostentatiously bought the entire stock with a large quantity of banknotes. Mrs Kernochan disapproved – this was not genteel behaviour. On arrival at the Hotel Bristol it was discovered that Emilie was using the suite normally occupied by the Prince of Wales. Mrs Kernochan, now highly suspicious, instituted enquiries, a result of which Emilie's invitation was withdrawn. She fought back and 'boldly claimed to be the [illegitimate] daughter of Mr Yerkes',[13] but to no avail. Towner says that she normally called Yerkes her 'uncle' in America and her 'guardian' in England, but if pressed would say he was her illegitimate father. Braxton called him Uncle Charley and the servants at Park Avenue called him Mr Grigsby. Yerkes led a complicated life, full of deception, and could have made a good secret agent.

Emilie Grigsby now had no hope of making a marriage at the comfort level to which Yerkes' money had accustomed – if not entitled – her. The probability, supported by Dreiser's version of events, is that she now 'surrendered' to him and became his mistress – a development which must have been highly satisfactory to him. It is not beyond the realms of possibility that he instigated the exposures to bring this about, given that he was ruthless enough to do so. As Dreiser puts it they were both 'social outcasts'.[15] Respectable social circles in and around Fifth Avenue were aware of the nature of her relationship to Yerkes.

To bear this out, after the brush with Mrs Kernochan – a police captain from Cincinnati had talked – a society hostess later said:

> I don't think anyone ever visited her after that. Everyone knew. She was pointed out at the opera, but no one ever went to her box.[16]

A rich aunt in Kentucky did not leave her any money, according to Towner, so it was easy to deduce that she was in disgrace and that Yerkes was the source of her wealth.[17]

The House of Mystery

'Strange tales were told of its concealed elevators and secret panels.'[18]

In about 1898, Yerkes purchased a mansion at 660 Park Avenue, for which he gave the deeds to Emilie. She was nineteen. It was in sight of 864 Fifth Avenue and called by the newspapers, gleefully but guardedly, the 'House of Mystery'. It was a narrow building, four or five storeys high, and alterations were made. It was not as grand as Yerkes' establishment; externally it was less impressive as it did not overlook Central Park and in front of it were blow-holes emitting smoke and steam from the trains of the New York Central Railroad. Nonetheless, inside, according to Towner, there was a 'churchly' atmosphere, with '. . . a waft of incense in the air, the soft prismatic twilight of jeweled lamps from an old Italian altar, the time worn glow of Persian rugs and old church vestments'. Woven into the rugs were sanctimonious questions like 'What says the lark to the rose in the garden?' and 'Why weary of life when everything is beautiful?' He says that Emilie became interested in the 'eternal struggle between Good and Evil'.[18] More conservatively, Philip Gerber describes it thus:

By common consensus, it was a palace, standing four stories tall on the corner of Sixtyseventh Street, with half a block of frontage on Park Avenue, not more than three blocks from Yerkes' own home. The interior was furnished with art trophies of Yerkes' foreign travels: rare porcelains, jades, and Tanagra figurines, Empire furniture, a vast collection of medieval ecclesiatical vestments sewn with jewels, and a library of 11,000 volumes. The white marble walls of its central hall were hung with Aubusson tapestries, its staircase dominated by Coppee's portrait of Emilie 'in clinging, sheer silks, with a toy dog jumping at her plump hand.'[20]

A year after moving in, Yerkes, generous as always, presented Emilie with an $85,000 piano. The reporter on the Chicago *Sunday Tribune* must have interviewed friends and servants, for after Yerkes' death he was able to write about the most intriguing feature of all: the bedroom. Emilie's appeared to be suitably chaste and religious – like a nun's cell with a narrow bed with a crucifix. However, there was a secret elevator which would take the robber baron up to a sumptuous apartment where Emilie could entertain him. Did he expect her to receive him if she had made a respectable marriage? Or would he have installed another mistress there? In any event he was disloyal to Emilie and had two other affairs after she took possession of the house.

Yerkes' personal life was undoubtedly busy, but to what extent the rumours reached England is not known. He never came to London alone; Emilie would accompany him but, for the sake of propriety on the high seas, on a separate steamer. Although on strained terms with his wife Mara, a suite at Claridges would be taken for her for the sake of appearances, yet on one occasion he paid a playboy to look after her in Paris whilst he entertained Gladys Unger in London (deceiving Emilie also). She was seventeen and he had taken an interest in her since 1896 when she was twelve. As with Emilie he had detected a long–term 'investment'. Gladys had a suite at the Hotel Cecil – where Yerkes stayed and conducted business meetings. It should be said that Gladys had creative talent and started as an artist but became a successful playwright. In

Above left: 1 A watercolour drawing of the Chicago elevated Loop, or 'L', at Van Buren Street, which opened in October 1897. (Courtesy New York Public Library)

Above right: 2 The Chicago Elevated in 2001. Judging by the length of the train it is heavily used. (Author's collection)

Above left: 3 Yerkes' Chicago Elevated at the intersection of Lake Street and Wells Street in 1900. The sharp curves at the Loop's access junctions reduced the number of trains per hour that could be operated. (Author's collection)

Above right: 4 Yerkes' Mansion was on Fifth Avenue, New York, and this drawing is called 'The Glory Of Fifth Avenue Inspires Even Those On Foot'. It is a winter scene drawn by Frank Craig (1874–1918). Fifth Avenue became known as Millionaires Row in the 1890s. (Picture courtesy of New York Public Library)

6 This photograph of Fifth Avenue at Thirty-First Street shows the Waldorf-Astoria Hotel which dominated the scene. It is here that Yerkes died. A few old residential properties are left among the shop fronts, shortly to be redeveloped and the scene transformed. (Picture courtesy of New York Public Library)

7 Electrified track at Earl's Court. The years 1897–1906 were a period of great upheaval in London, involving the construction of a rapid transit system comparable to that enjoyed by Boston and being constructed in Paris, Berlin, and New York. The electrification of the District railway seemed a complex, if not insuperable problem, but was accomplished by Yerkes and completed in less than three years. So far, as is known, there were virtually no interruptions in service, the work being done at night. This photograph, of indifferent quality, was taken early in 1905, some months before electrified services started, and shows the conductor rails which have been laid at the western end of Earl's Court. The line to Hammersmith, which was opened in 1874, diverges to the left of the picture and the line to West Brompton of 1869 diverges to the right. To the left of the Hammersmith lines, but out of frame, is the sub-station to which current was fed from Lot's Road power house at 11,000v ac and reduced to 600v dc for distribution to the system. In the late 1890s it had seemed easier to build a tube and the District obtained powers for a deep-level line from Earl's Court to Charing Cross; under Yerkes, the section from Earl's Court to South Kensington was united with the Brompton & Piccadilly Circus tube, and was the genesis of the Piccadilly line. When this photograph was taken this tube railway extended back to Hammersmith, beneath the lines shown here, and was nearly completed. (Photograph: *Tramway and Railway World*)

Opposite above: 5 In the early 1890s Yerkes decided to build a mansion in New York to demonstrate his wealth, and also perhaps because he sensed 'that all his worlds were temporary and that the least temporary might be one where he was not responsible for the discomfort of the straphangers', says Wesley Towner. The mansion, expanded by stages with progress being reported by the *New York Times*, occupied more ground than any other building on Fifth Avenue. Amongst the opulence and ostentation were 'halls of mirrors, halls of marble, halls of story-painted panels dwelling on the pleasures of the flesh ... [and] ... a Louis XV room, an East Indian room, a Japanese room, an Empire room transported from France with its boiserie and furnishings intact.' It couldn't have been in more questionable taste: 'The two long picture galleries were simple and uncluttered, but the third, and largest, gallery – on the Fifth Avenue side, with an entrance from the street – boasted a marble staircase. Here were the sculptures – groups by Rodin and figures by Hondon, mingled, alas! with a ghostly community of of 8-foot maidens en route to the bath.' Here is a view of Fifth Avenue in the 1900s – a street that New York was immensely proud of. The artist has included motor cars and motor buses mingling with horse-drawn traffic. (Picture courtesy of New York Public Library)

8 Earl's Court station, District railway, following electrification, and with new platforms. Signs direct passengers to the 'moving stairway' to the Piccadilly tube, the first in use on the system. Also in place are electrical indicators showing which trains are arriving. (London Transport Museum. 1999/20030)

9 It has recently come to light that Yerkes' mansion was bought by a Mr Ryan for $1.2 million in 1908 and then demolished. The site was turned into a garden. Mr Ryan lived at 858 on Fifth Avenue. This is a recent apartment block at the corner of Fifth Avenue and East 68 Street where Yerkes' mansion may have stood. It is a far cry from the closing years of the nineteenth century. This is facing Central Park. (Photograph: Bruce Rankin)

10 District railway. 0-4-4T steam locomotive No.4 at East Ham in about 1905, on the Wimbledon service, shortly before electrification. Although electrified services were running to Wimbledon from 27 August 1905, steam traction continued on the District for a few more months until November. Posing for the photographer is Driver Yates and his fireman, Mr Hutchings, who was his son-in-law. (London Transport Museum. 1998/59655)

11 The pre-Yerkes era: a steam-hauled District train for Wimbledon entering Putney Bridge station, probably in the 1890s. Note the wooden platforms (which had to be removed for electrification as they were considered a fire risk by the Board of Trade), the signal box and the semaphore signals. These were replaced after electrification in 1905. Note also the advertisement for Australian wine, suggesting that its popularity is not as recent as supposed. (Author's collection)

12 Yerkes' American railway. The revolutionary 'cars' of American design, designated as B stock, posed here probably on the Ealing & South Harrow railway. They had sliding doors and longitudinal seating with plenty of room for standing passengers, for whom leather straps were provided. There is no record of Yerkes saying that the straphangers in London would be paying his dividends. (London Transport Museum. 24117)

13 Stairwell entrance on the concourse of Euston station to the separate stations of the City & South London and Charing Cross and Hampstead tubes in 1915. The former had been absorbed into the Underground Group on 1 January 1913, having been weakened by bus competition. The rail connection to the Charing Cross was opened in 1924 by means of an extension from Euston to Camden Town. It later became known as the Northern line. Information about fares is clearly provided, including important stations on another Underground line – the Great Northern Piccadilly & Brompton. Yerkes had advocated a flat fare of 2d, a principle which had been successfully adopted in the USA. (London Transport Museum. 1998/58672)

14 By November 1904 the Metropolitan Railway had completed the electrification of their new line to Uxbridge. Trial runs were made from Baker Street on 17th and 22nd of that month. These were satisfactory. This photograph is of the demonstration run for the press which was laid on for 13 December. The line was passed by the Board of Trade Inspector on 15 December, and the service opened to the public on 1 January 1905. In this the Metropolitan was six months ahead of Yerkes' District lines. (London Transport Museum. 1998/59669)

15 An Edwardian summer's day at Southfields between Wimbledon and Putney Bridge not long after electrification. A train of B stock is arriving in this rural setting; electrification probably hastened house development in this area. (Pat Loobey collection)

Opposite top: 16 Earl's Court station. A posed photograph looking west, taken in 1905 after the electrification of the District track had been completed and before the Piccadilly line had opened. Work is in progress on the replacement of the wooden platforms by concrete, the Board of Trade having required the use of less flammable material. Ducts for cabling were laid beneath them. The same requirement had been stipulated for the sleepers where non-flammable hardwood from Australia was used. By today's standards there are few passengers around. The newly installed destination indicators with blue enamel name places can be seen over the far platform – these are still in use to this day. The sign above them, slightly out of focus, says: 'TO THE FIELDS AND FRESH AIR. AN IDEAL SUNDAY AFTERNOON EXCURSION. HARROW RETURN FARE 8d 4 TRAINS HOURLY.' This refers to the Ealing & South Harrow line which had been used as a test bed for electrification, and ran through open country. It is now the Piccadilly line to Rayners Lane. (London Transport Museum. 1998/88884)

Opposite centre: 17 Baker Street & Waterloo. A drawing published by *The Graphic* on 17 March 1906 of Trafalgar Square station (now Charing Cross) on the opening day (10 March). This was almost exactly four years after Yerkes obtained control of this line, on which construction had halted as result of the collapse of the London & Globe Finance Corporation. Stations were designed by Leslie Green and many provided with large electric clocks and garden seats, clearly shown here. It was the first of Yerkes' tube railways to open. (London Transport Museum. 1998/75633)

Opposite below: 18 Great Northern, Piccadilly & Brompton. Yerkes merged the Brompton & Piccadilly and the Great Northern & Strand to provide a meaningful route through central London, which quickly became known as the Piccadilly line when it was extended west to Hammersmith. 218 cars were ordered and this photograph is of one of two cars built in Britain which were too large and therefore not used. The rest were built in France and Hungary and had transverse and longitudinal seats with leather straps for standing passengers. The line opened on 15 December 1906. (London Transport Museum 1998/84219)

Previous page, below: 19 Tottenham Court Road station. A photograph taken on a cold and cloudy day in January 1923. It is where the Central London line and Yerkes' Charing Cross and Hampstead tube cross. This entrance, in Oxford Street, is to the Hampstead line station, which opened in June 1907, seven years after the Central London line station. For the first year of operation this station was called Oxford Street but the inevitable confusion necessitated a change of name. The station to the north had been called Tottenham Court Road and this was changed to Goodge Street. There were no surface buildings for the Hampstead line station because land was not available, but there was a connecting passage between the two stations and a public subway. This station contained the typical features of Yerkes' stations; these included Otis electric lifts with a spiral iron staircase for emergency use, from the subterranean booking hall; separate station tunnels; stone-edged concrete platforms, each of which had a large electric clock and garden seats; platform walls lined with tiles of a unique colour, enabling regular travellers to recognise each station (if they could not see the station name). Back at street level the wooden canopy protected the stairs from rain and the decorative ironwork is impressive, enhancing the landscape of the street. It had to attract the tourist and the shopper as a means of moving around London. It became a heavily used station and stops had to be extended from 20 to 35–40 seconds. The Central London was taken over by the Underground Group in 1913. Of interest is the elaborately designed lamppost and the No.19 bus, an S-type. (London Transport Museum. 1998/58613)

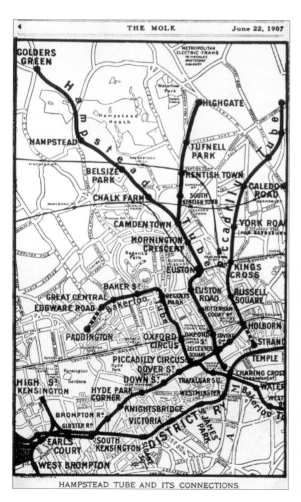

20 The Yerkes tubes. A map from the magazine *The Mole* of 22 June 1907, the opening day of the Hampstead Tube as it was called, which depicts not only the CCEH but the other Yerkes' tube railways, the Bakerloo and the GNPBR – already called the Piccadilly. On this railway, Dover Street station was renamed Green Park in 1933, Down Street closed in 1932 and Brompton Road closed in 1934. The Central London is discernible, as is the Waterloo & City, but the Metropolitan and the Circle are not shown, to prevent the map being overcrowded. The Bakerloo did not reach Paddington until 1913. (London Transport Museum. 1998/2887)

21 The Hampstead Tube. An example of publicity produced for the opening of the Charing Cross and Hampstead tube on 22 June 1907. It can be seen that the progression from the centre of London at Charing Cross to the rural charm of Golders Green and Highgate is considered a strong selling point, hence the statement 'To country homes', aimed at the potential commuter. The line was extended back to Embankment in 1914. What was then called Highgate was in fact Archway and the line was not extended to Highgate until 1939. The interchange with main line services at Euston is also emphasized by the illustration of the Doric arch, which was demolished when Euston was rebuilt in 1962–68. (London Transport Museum. 2002/9758)

22 The tube railways were new and were not yet part of the fabric of London, so they had to draw attention to themselves. One way to do this was to have prominent entrances which provided as much accessible information as possible. This is Trafalgar Square, now Charing Cross, in about 1907. Note that the shortened name of Bakerloo has already been officially adopted for the Baker Street and Waterloo Railway, which opened from those two destinations on 10 March 1906. (London Transport Museum. 1998/87172)

Above left: 23 The Kentucky Beauty. This portrait was published by the Chicago *Daily Tribune* on 3 January 1906, five days after Yerkes' demise. He had been successful in suppressing details of his private life, but after his death newspapers felt free to release the stories they had filed away and the public were inundated with the backlog. Articles were headed by sensational statements such as 'Emilie Grigsby, Beautiful Kentucky Girl, Maintained for Years in Oriental Splendor'. Emilie was in London in 1901 for the coronation of Edward VII and was accompanied by Mrs Ellen Dunlap Hopkins of New York, who subsequently told a reporter, 'I think she was the most beautiful woman I ever saw. Her eyes were brown. Her hair had the reddish gleam of gold. Her face sad in expression. Her complexion like alabaster. Her form was beautiful.' (Author's collection)

Above right: 24 A pen and wash cartoon by Max Beerbohm, entitled 'One of Our Conquerers'. It depicts Yerkes. (London Transport Museum. 1998/52441)

25 Hamilton House on Victoria Embankment, which was completed in 1901, and became the headquarters of Underground Electric Railways of London – known as the Underground Group – when formed the following year. This was a holding company which controlled Yerkes' companies and about which London financial circles and the London County Council had misgivings. (Bruce Rankin)

The (Monroe) D(octrine) Railway.
BROTHER JONATHAN to METROPOLITAN RAILWAY : "Well, whatever your Company may
do, I reckon I mean to keep this bit for myself"

Above left: 26 Doris Keane, born in Michigan in 1881. She was on the Chicago stage before moving to London in 1907. In the portrait above she plays Margherita Cavallini in *Romance*. This opened in 1915 and ran for 1,049 performances, raising her to stardom. Her one venture into Shakespeare was as Juliet, with Ellen Terry as the nurse and Basil Sydney as Romeo. This was at the Lyric Theatre and ran for seventy-three performances. Her relationship with Yerkes must have been in the late 1890s, before either of them moved to London. Shane Leslie speculates in his autobiography, *Long Shadows*, that she was expected to be one of the main beneficiaries of Yerkes' will. In *The Elegant Auctioneers*, Wesley Towner says that Yerkes' mistresses in Chicago consisted, inter alia, of 'stenographers and actresses, and young girls being trained for the stage', one of the latter becoming a 'famous star'. ['Autumn on a nest egg stemming from Chicago's streetcars.'] The Chicago papers in the 1890s carried pictures of his mistresses. (Commercial postcard)

Above right: 27 A satirical drawing which appeared in the *Railway Magazine* in 1901, expressing the concern felt about American investment in England – in this case the District railway – which was now controlled by Charles Tyson Yerkes. (Author's collection)

28 Yerkes photographed on 17 November 1900, aged sixty-three. This portrait was clearly intended to reassure the creditors and shareholders, but he had been called, amongst other things, 'the rascally American financier'. He was indifferent to insults and had his admirers; for example the journal *Tramway & Railway World*, which said that he was 'the soul of honour'. This periodical reported that Yerkes did not drink alcohol or tea, did not smoke and it said that his face was 'pale ... almost sallow ... with a singularly agreeable smile'. Is this what women found attractive, or was it mainly the money? (London Transport Museum. 1998/57854)

Above left: 29 Edgar Speyer. A portrait made as a young man before he became a baronet. Yerkes had said 'In business we always have to take chances but I believe this is the best chance I ever took'. Speyer's decision to back him must have been a source of great regret when neither the electrification of the District railway nor the construction of the tubes yielded the revenue which had been predicted. (London Transport Museum. 1998/40806)

Above right: 30 R.W. Perks. The devout Methodist who encouraged Yerkes to modernise London's transport. He had invested heavily in the District railway and realized that he would only get a return if it was electrified. Electrification was delayed, firstly by the technical dispute with the Metropolitan Railway, and then by late deliveries from suppliers. As company chairman, Perks had the unenviable job of mollifying the shareholders at biannual company meetings. Many of them had not received a dividend since 1882. It was claimed, somewhat doubtfully, that Yerkes/UERL did not have a majority holding. (London Transport Museum. 1998/40826)

32 Hotel Cecil. A 1923 view of the Strand, looking east, with the Vaudeville Theatre on the left and the Hotel Cecil on the right. This was where Yerkes stayed and conducted business until UERL opened their headquarters further along the Embankment. One of his mistresses, Gladys Unger, also had a suite of rooms here until she moved into a Mayfair flat. The Hotel Cecil opened in 1886 with 800 rooms, and was the largest hotel in Europe, renowned for its opulence. It was popular with rich Americans. It was on the site of Shell-Mex House which was built in 1931. (London Transport Museum. 1999/3225)

Opposite below: 31 Experimental electric stock which ran between Earl's Court and High Street Kensington from November 1899, and then in public service from 21 May 1900 at a special fare of 1s (5p) per journey. It consisted of six coaches, with seats for 312 passengers, and weighed 185 tons. The two end coaches had Siemens motors which were supplied with 500 volts d.c. current by two conductor rails outside the running rails. The route was considered appropriate as it consisted of gradients and curves, over which the train's performance was satisfactory. The Metropolitan and the District allocated £20,000 for these trials but there was an over-run of £2,000. S.B. Fortenbaugh, one of the experienced electrical engineers who was brought over from the USA by Yerkes, later said that this experiment was 'very costly', given that d.c. systems had been in successful commercial operation at Chicago since 1895 and Boston since 1898. The District railway claimed that one reason for the trials was to see if electric and steam trains could be operated concurrently. It was certainly a delaying tactic. Despite the development of electric traction in the USA and Germany, railway managers in Britain were wedded to steam. As one of the historians of the Metropolitan Railway has put it, 'It was not thought feasible that an agency so unaccountable and mysterious [electricity], could ever be employed in a mechanical form'. (London Transport Museum. 1998/87082)

33 Lots Road power station. Called both a 'monument to Yerkes' and the 'Chelsea Monster', this aerial view shows the excellent position with access from river and rail. The land was bought by the Brompton & Piccadilly Railway and the project taken over by Yerkes for the supply of electricity to the Underground Group. It was designed by the chief engineer, William Russell Chapman, who had twenty-seven-years' experience of electrical engineering on railways in the USA. It was the first all-turbine power station, with the largest turbines of the time, and construction started in 1902. It was commissioned three years later. Although the river bank had become industrialised, there were objections to the power station, notably from the American painter James McNeil Whistler, whose painting 'Nocturne in Black and Gold: The Falling Rocket' was involved in Whistler's libel action against John Ruskin. The painting was about Cremorne Pleasure Gardens, which had been situated here until closed in 1877.

Cremorne was on the edge of the built-up area, and succumbed to pressure from moralists, magistrates, and the relentless advance of metropolitan London. A small garden area and one of the garden's gates have been restored on the site. The power station was decommissioned in 2002 and is being converted to luxury flats. (London Transport Museum. 2004/15913) the early 1900s she moved out of the Hotel Cecil, and took a house in Charles Street, Mayfair, which was full of Yerkes' pictures and antiques; various people were aware of her relationship with Yerkes. She is mentioned by Sir Shane Leslie in his memoirs. On a money-raising trip to New York, Yerkes had another affair, this time with Ethel Link Yerkes, a great-niece.

Yerkes probably wanted to leave his wife, but Mara would not have agreed. A divorce at this time would have created a scandal and he was an outsider already and did not want to go too far beyond the pale. A high-profile divorce with his sexual adventures being aired in court might have been too much for the bankers (they had always been willing to lend him money but never to take him home to meet their wives). So appearances were maintained and Yerkes had to be content with discreet visits to various hotels and the House of Mystery.

All sources agree that Emilie was a woman of exceptional beauty (she became known in some circles as the 'Kentucky Beauty')[21] and that to Yerkes she was a beautiful possession more desirable than the Rembrandts, but like them she was a gilt-edged investment. Mrs Dunlap Hopkins said, 'She was the most beautiful woman I ever saw.'[22] The Chicago *Sunday Tribune* raved about her, saying that she was:

> ...a girl whom any person in the street would turn and stare at, involuntarily. Tall, of an ideal figure, she had a wonderful alabasterlike complexion which any woman might envy. Her reddish hair was a striking feature. She had the carriage and style to which men apply the admiring word 'thoroughbred'. She dressed in perfect taste, with an individuality of style that made whatever fashion which she adopted seemed to be the last triumph of art in clothes.[23]

In addition to her good looks she possessed, according to all sources, charm and personality. Towner, whilst scathing about every aspect of Yerkes' life, is gushing in his praise of Emilie (though so far, as is known, he had not actually met her):

Her marvelous red-gold hair would have defied the brush of Titian, a number of admirers said; no angel of the golden ages had been depicted with such purity of alabaster skin; the ever-changing sea itself could not aspire to the azure softness of her languid eyes; nor could the sorrows of the Muses describe the peculiarly mournful expression beneath their heavy lids. There were others who said she was proud and cold, like a diamond in disposition, but most of those who saw her were inarticulate with wonder. They simply said she was a poem.[24]

Emilie in London

'There are only two crimes in Society: one to be poor, the other to be found out.'[25]

In Dreiser's books, the character of Berenice Fleming is based on Emilie Grigsby and was sufficiently realistic to delay publication of *The Titan*. In this, Berenice encourages Cowperwood/Yerkes to move to London and it is very probable that this is based on real life. Given that Emilie had no future in the upper levels of New York society, she would have reasoned that she might succeed in London, where little was known about her. It is also certain that, despite the difference in their ages, she had some influence over him; in 1900 she was a mature twenty-one year old, and Yerkes was a less-than-mature sixty-four year old. It is therefore likely that she strengthened his inclination to undertake the modernization of London's urban railway system. He was a restless man with great mental energy who was not yet ready for retirement. This would be his last, triumphant project, which would teach the aldermen in Chicago a lesson – he would join the top rank of robber barons. But time was running out; by this time he was losing his impressive appearance. He was no longer handsome, had put on weight and was going grey – all the things he could not forgive in a woman.

Emilie's strategy was correct, up to a point. She found an arena for her charm and social graces and may have played some sort of role as a

Mayfair hostess in Edwardian London. One cannot be absolutely defi-
nite but it is unlikely that she would have reached the highest circles and
rubbed shoulders with the very best people – although Towner thinks
she was presented to Edward VII, which was quite possible as he had a
liking for nouveaux riches like Yerkes.

However, for Yerkes, she facilitated introductions, in a milieu which
tended to be hostile. Towner says, 'Her beauty and her sables, her white-
washed pedigree, and her mythical Southern fortune, opened doors that
Yerkes could never have entered except as her guardian.'[26]

Yerkes bought her a house in Brook Street, Mayfair:

> . . . where she gave stately dinners to the investors. When she appeared
> at a party in a clinging white satin robe, with a sapphire at her neck an
> inch and a half square, the monied world professed with one accord
> never to have set eyes on a creature so ravishing.[27]

She was in London for the coronation of Edward VII in 1901. A con-
temporary source on Emilie's appearance was Mrs Ellen Dunlap
Hopkins, founder of the New York School of Applied Design for
Women, whose students had made copies of some of Yerkes' tapestries.
She was Emilie's official chaperone at the time of the coronation and
told reporters:

> The girl to me was a poem, I think she was the most beautiful woman
> I ever saw . . . I think Mr Yerkes in her had the great passion of his life.
> He just worshipped her, that's all.[28]

Despite using the word 'passion', Mrs Hopkins later claimed, rather
coyly, that she did not know exactly what Emilie's relationship with
Yerkes was, and that she was not a chaperone. But she could not afford
to make an enemy of Yerkes. Nonetheless, she related that when Emilie
'graduated' from her convent, the Mother Superior told her about her
mother's life 'and that it was her duty to reclaim her'.[29] In penance, Sue
Grigsby somewhat excessively made pilgrimages to Rome.

Dreiser summarised Mrs Hopkins' remarks:

> [Emilie's] eyes were brown. Her hair had the reddish gleam of gold. Her face sad in expression. Her complexion like alabaster. Her form was beautiful. She was not more than five feet five inches tall but she wore, usually, clinging soft white robes that seemed to give her height. I remember distinctly once . . . seeing her in long white robes adorned with ropes of faint pink coral and I thought her the most beautiful creature I had ever seen.[30]

For the 1901 London 'season' Emilie was also accompanied by another American, Miss Eleanor Green. A London newspaper was quoted as describing Emilie as a 'charming, beautiful and extremely wealthy New Yorker' in possession of £20,000 per year in her own right, and an ardent Roman Catholic. On arriving in London she announced that she was going into a convent. This was a useful ploy as it would have forestalled questions and created sympathy.

The Chicago *Sunday Tribune* explained that she was able to pursue her harmless ambitions in London, because there is a 'certain grade of society in the British capital to which unaccredited women of wealth are received, and her successes in this circle were gratifying to her, while they made her discontented with her New York failures'.[31]

Yerkes' first year in London (1901) was a busy year; he bought Emilie a summer retreat, a house on the Thames at Maidenhead called 'The Chalet'. Here she gave parties, with mixed results. At luncheon on the lawn Emilie shocked her guests when, 'holding her soft, clinging dress tightly about her, she proceeded to swing and sway gracefully around in a circle, to the horrified surprise of the entire party'. The guests abandoned dancing after this. The incident hardly seems shocking to us, but it breached the social conventions of the time.[32]

But according to Towner, who was not afraid to exaggerate, she was a sensation:

From Mayfair to the Riviera, Miss Emilie became known almost overnight as the Kentucky Beauty. It was reported that a Prince Windischgratz of Hungary was engaged to marry her, likewise Prince Deldrago of Italy.[33]

Much of Towner's information must be based on gossip columns and is therefore unreliable. He mentions the *Daily Tribune* which, in its obituary of 30 December 1905, said that Yerkes was 'admitted to the old aristocratic society' in London, a typical Americanism which should not be taken literally.

If Yerkes lived in the present age, much of his time would be spent on a jet aeroplane. But he lived in a more elegant age (for the rich) and resided on ocean liners and luxury trains. If Emilie was accompanying him they would be discreet; they used separate steamers when crossing the Atlantic. Yerkes was often met by reporters when disembarking at Southampton and he needed to avoid scandal in London. When he went to Italy and Hungary to inspect the Ganz electrical system in the summer of 1901, it is possible that he combined this with a stay on the Italian lakes with Emilie as his companion. This is no more than conjecture, however, because there is no evidence to support it, and she may have spent that summer at Maidenhead (or she may have been back in New York). Also, it would have been less than discreet because he had colleagues with him.

In Dreiser's final volume of the trilogy *The Stoic*, Berenice's mother (Sue Grigsby) fears in England that exposure of their background could come from visiting Americans, and this did indeed happen. In 1911, when she had returned after Yerkes' death and a trip to India, Emilie claimed that she was acquainted with the governess of Queen Mary's daughter, the Princess Royal, aged fourteen, and that the Princess herself had befriended her. As a result Emilie claimed that she was offered a seat in Westminster Abbey for the Coronation of George V on 22 June 1911. For good measure, she also said that she had shared a box with 'royalty' at the opera (it is not clear exactly who she meant). The London correspondent of the *New York Times* duly sent this information to his paper which was printed with some incredulity: how had Queen Mary taken a liking to her when she was not admitted to New York society? The report included, however, the sceptical comment of an unnamed American in London:

> The Lady of the House of Mystery in Park Avenue now dates her correspondence from Buckingham Palace. To the ward of a Chicago street railway magnate who burrowed underground in London has been alloted a place in the royal box at the Westminster Abbey coronation ceremony.[34]

This was followed two days later by an anonymous letter in support of Emilie – she had been taught 'modest dignity' at her convent, she had been taught southern manners, her father having been a commander of Federal (Union) troops in the Civil War, and 'her success in England must be accepted as a tribute to individual merit'.[35] Was this sent by one of Yerkes' agents?

A week later, the *New York Times*, which had been duped to some extent, printed the angry revelation under the front-page headline: 'MISS GRIGSBY DREW A VERY LONG BOW'. Emilie had not been invited to the Coronation, nor invited to Buckingham Palace, and whoever had let her in by the backstairs was now in trouble and likely to lose their job. An investigation was under way. The article continued:

> To the world at large, of course, it is a matter of no consequence whether Miss Grigsby was in the Abbey or not, but as her romances give rise to gossip reflecting on the perspecuity and good sense of Queen Mary, it is merely an act of justice to give as wide publicity to the real facts as the Grigsbian fiction has received. . .
>
> That the gates of Buckingham Palace were thrown open to the American visitor, whose shadow never darkened the doors of her own countrywomen of light and leading, is true only so far as this, that Miss Grigsby's entree was of the backstairs variety. . .

Miss Grigsby's 'social success' proves on investigation to be an equally baseless fabric of the imagination.[36]

Behind this lies the jostling and competition amongst upper-class Americans for places in Westminster Abbey and at other social gatherings. When Emilie's pretensions became blatant, they would have been quick to apprise London society of her relationship with Yerkes, as well as her mother's profession. As Towner says, 'Veracity was not one of her strong points.'[37]

A similar incident occurred years later, which is recounted by Sir Shane Leslie:

It was creditable to Emilie that the Princess Royal could enjoy her friendship at one time. They appeared in public until espied by two American ladies who informed Queen Mary that Miss Grigsby was no proper companion for a King's daughter. The friendship was checked. It was creditable to the Princess that she sent Emilie an invitation to her wedding, in fact several, for Queen Mary tore them up! Finally the Princess insisted and an invitation to the Abbey appeared on Emilie's mantel. Emilie had the tact not to go.[38]

The Princess Royal was married in 1922. Emilie would never give up.

When Emilie arrived at New York in September 1911 on the *Olympic*, after the Coronation episode, accompanied by a maid and manservant, reporters clamoured to question her. But she refused interviews and the manservant stood guard outside her stateroom door. Instead, she gained more notoriety when hostile customs officers spent an hour examining her jewels, which she valued at $800,000. These, she claimed, were given to her before she had left the USA and included three pearl strings, one of which had nearly 100 pearls and was worth $200,000. Her baggage consisted of fourteen trunks and eleven small pieces of luggage, containing sixty 'handsome gowns'.[39] Her life at this time was full of such newsworthy incidents.

The contents of the Park Avenue mansion were auctioned in January 1912, and realised $193,067 – substantially less than the $2 million for the paintings, rugs, and sculptures at Yerkes' mansion. After the sale of the building (it is not clear when), Emilie travelled to India. Gerber says that Dreiser noted a newspaper report (but does not say which one) on 13 January 1913 of her departure from Paris for India to study yogi philosophy, and quoting, 'For several years, since the fiasco of her social aspirations at the time of King George's coronation, she has taken a great interest in the Yogi philosophers'.[40] The report concludes, cruelly, by saying that this may console her in the light of her 'waning beauty'. She would now have been in her mid-thirties.

Philip Gerber points out that Emilie was as materialistic as her benefactor and far from unselfish. He quotes Mrs Hopkins who was reported by the Chicago *Daily Tribune* as saying,: 'She is not given to great generosities. I never heard of her giving away anything but old clothes.' She sold off her 'loot', not for money, but for revenge on the men who had sought her favours with such gifts. 'Nearly all these men are among the dollar princes of the world. They must bid high to gain back the gifts that they gave her.'[41]

But Emilie returned to England to resume a quieter life. To what extent she re-established herself is uncertain. By some she was just accepted as 'mysterious' and rich. Calling herself an heiress explained away her wealth. Her friends seemed to have been men who were intrigued by her personality and her beauty. She lived in Mayfair and at a Tudor cottage at West Drayton, which before the First World War was still an unspoilt rural retreat (it is now close to Heathrow airport). When she died in 1964, an anonymous tribute was published in *The Times*, which described her as a 'mysterious and beautiful figure' from New York who became an 'Edwardian hostess . . . who deserves memory in any record of Mayfair in its most brilliant phase'.[42] Like much of Towner's material, it is a mixture of fact and fantasy which Emilie had surrounded herself in for the whole of her life. The author (probably Sir Shane Leslie) claims that she was painted by the court painter of Emperor Francis Joseph of Austria, 'an honour she shared in America with Mr Rockefeller alone'. This may be part of what the *New York Times* called (in 1911) the 'Grigsbian fiction'.[43]

The tribute goes on to say that Emilie aimed at a salon in Mayfair which became 'an exquisite dining saloon', and that society was nervous of accepting her, but she 'could out-entertain her rivals with wines and cooking beyond their ken', her soup having twenty-six ingredients. She looked on herself as the 'mascot of the high command during the First World War', Old Meadows, being at their disposal where she 'entertained warriors in need of rest or private conference'. Indeed, on one occasion it is claimed that Sir John French and Lord Kitchener met there 'while sentries ensured seclusion'. This is again dubious given that French and Kitchener were not on speaking terms. It is also claimed that Rupert Brooke spent his last night in England there, and 'the lines he wrote were afterwards engraved in bronze over the door'. Finally, we are told that Emilie's pale beauty and golden hair 'very slowly faded'. What is striking in terms of transport history is that the tribute contains no reference to Charles Tyson Yerkes. The past is well and truly buried. But her life can hardly have been carefree as she must have been in fear of exposure.

Emilie appears in the memoirs of Sir Shane Leslie, who also calls her 'mysterious', and remembers her as a Mayfair hostess. Sir Shane says that Emilie 'sometimes whispered about her wonderful past – especially when she wished her fairy story told in a book'.[44] Parts of her past may have been wonderful, and no doubt she was selective. Yerkes is referred to as 'Colonel' Yerkes, so one can surmise that the robber baron used this title to attain more respectability in London society. Her relationship with him is implied when Leslie says that the fortune was divided between Emilie, Gladys Unger and Doris Keane – the last being a successful Chicago actress, born in 1881, portraits of whom can be seen at www.npg.ac.uk in the collection of the National Portrait Gallery, London.

According to Sir Shane, Emilie believed she was sculptured in Rodin's *Baiser*, and claimed that Meredith had foreseen her as Lucy Feverel. She claimed that Yeats had admired her. She also claimed, according to Sir Shane, that she had recovered love letters which Queen Marie of Romania had written to an American. She claimed, furthermore, that she had 'entertained the military luxuriously' during the First World

War. In addition to French, Sir John Cowans, Quartermaster-General, was a guest, as was Colonel Repington, *The Times'* war correspondent, who was 'madly in love' with her. At Old Meadows, French, Repington and Lord Northcliffe met 'to make a certainty on the military side of Asquith's fall from the Premiership'. Emilie told stories of her travels in India, where she was accompanied by servants. According to Sir Shane she was nicknamed the 'Undressed Salad' by her British acquaintances, which strongly suggests that her reputation was raffish; her friends and acquaintances in England were men of the world who were unconcerned about this and probably intrigued.[45]

Sir Shane Leslie was a Catholic Irish baronet who had American relatives and was a first cousin of Sir Winston Churchill on his mother's side. It is possible that he may have only been on the fringes of the upper levels of society himself. He corresponded with Emilie and died in 1971. Clearly, his memoirs cannot be regarded as reliable evidence, but his son John says he recalls Emilie visiting the family home in Ireland in 1929. She arrived in a Rolls-Royce with a chauffeur and maid, together with Vyvyan Holland, the son of Oscar Wilde. Sir John Leslie must be one of the very few remaining people who can claim to have met her.

Emilie still had a flat in Mayfair – at 3 Curzon Place – but by the late 1950s there were complaints about the condition of the property and reports of both her and her maid, Willina Chisolm, drinking heavily. In 1960, Lord Southborough (who must have been a family friend and who had been a director of Shell Oil), was appointed her Receiver by the Court of Protection on grounds of Emilie's 'mental infirmity'. She bequeathed the West Drayton cottage to the National Trust, and took up residence in the Regents Park Nursing Home at 22 St Edmunds Terrace, NW8, where according to the tribute in *The Times*, she was forgotten by 'those she had generously adopted in the past'. The nursing home must have consumed some of her capital – the bills were about £65 per week – and a modest income was derived at this time from American stocks and shares. If she had had any UERL bonds they would have been realised in 1933 or 1947. The nursing home was demolished in the 1970s and has been replaced by a block of flats. On her death certificate she is described as a spinster which means that although she outlived Yerkes by fifty-nine years, she never married, at least in Britain.[46]

Other Mistresses

As already noted, Yerkes was not only physically attractive, but was considered a sparkling conversationalist and knew how to flatter women and make them feel good about themselves. However, with no diary and letters destroyed after his death, this aspect of his life is not documented. When Theodore Dreiser researched his novels he gleaned some information and this he used, with slight embellishment, in the second volume of the trilogy, *The Titan.*

W.A. Swanberg says that when Dreiser was researching for *The Titan* he found that Yerkes was:

> . . . charming, a fine conversationalist, a cunning predator who pursued women who had brains as well as beauty and broke with them kindly when he tired of them. When one of them took to the law, he would hire a man to romance with her, contrive to compromise her, and then Yerkes would threaten to expose her if she persisted. On his staff he had a battery of fifteen lawyers drawing something like $150,000 a year to protect him from women and other threats. . . [47]

Swanberg explains that Dreiser admired Yerkes/Cowperwood, knowing that he was a crook, 'but how strong, how able, how to get things done! If he was cruel, he was also the fittest and therefore entitled to survive.'[48]

Yerkes had to pay off his mistresses – they wouldn't leave him – why should they? A lot of his money (the fares paid by the Chicago straphangers) was spent in this way. It seems that if they were particularly obstinate, he would have a young man hired who would involve himself with them so that he could then accuse them of infidelity. There is no doubt that Yerkes was oversexed; the Fifth Avenue Mansion contained sculptures of naked women throughout the house.

The one Chicago mistress of whom there is a record is Clara Louise Hyllested. She was born in New York in 1865, the daughter of German immigrant parents, and married a pianist of some renown; she was beautiful and passionate. She and her husband came to Chicago in 1885 and Yerkes met them in the early 1890s, probably at a concert – he was fond of music.

Their affair lasted possibly from 1894 until 1897, her husband being on an extended European tour. When he heard of her infidelity he left her. Although Yerkes' passion cooled he maintained her in a luxurious apartment in Chicago for many years. As with others, he may have had difficulty in ending the relationship. Clara had plenty of spirit, and said (but Franch does not give his source or say where), 'When I find a personality that interests me . . . I am not easily driven from the battlefield, and I refuse to be cast off as a soiled and broken toy'.[49] She divorced in 1908, Hyllested retired to Scotland, and, according to Franch, Clara went to the worse and became a globe-trotting courtesan.

Doris Keane was a successful Chicago actress, born in about 1881 (died in 1945). She may have come to London and known Yerkes here, but she certainly consorted with him in Chicago. There are references in the Yerkes literature to a young girl who became a famous star and this may well have been Doris Keane. Her repertoire included Shakespeare and she received critical acclaim for her Juliet.

Although on strained terms with Mara, a suite at Claridges was taken for her for the sake of appearances, and he even hired a playboy to look after his estranged wife in Paris whilst he courted Gladys Unger in London (concurrently deceiving Emilie). This was in 1901 when by day he was grappling with the Metropolitan Railway over electrification. Gladys was seventeen, born in San Francisco in about 1885, and trained in London and Paris to be an artist. She obtained an honourable mention in the Paris salon of 1900. On returning to London she gave up art and became a playwright, her debut being a one-act play which was put on at the Vaudeville in the Strand. Yerkes had taken an interest in her since 1896 when she was eleven. As with Emilie he had spotted a long-term investment. Gladys had a suite at the Hotel Cecil (opposite the Vaudeville), where Yerkes stayed and rented rooms for business meetings. In the early 1900s Gladys Unger moved out of the Hotel Cecil and occupied a house in Charles Street, Mayfair. Her house was full of Yerkes' pictures and antiques; some members of London society were aware of her situation because she is mentioned by Sir Shane Leslie in his memoirs. In 1902 he agreed to provide her with an annual income of $5,000 for life. She was tall and dark-haired (unfortunately no pictures of her are available). She made a claim on Yerkes' estate in March 1907 at Cook County Probate Court, Chicago. She wrote over twenty plays and two books, before dying in 1940.

On a money-raising trip to New York, Yerkes had another affair, this time with Ethel Link Yerkes, a great-niece, with whom he was caught in King Otto's bed in the Fifth Avenue Mansion by Mara. Ethel was said to be Yerkes' favourite during the last year of his life. Her father had bolted to avoid an arrest warrant and her mother, penniless, had appealed to Yerkes, who rescued them. Ethel was a singer or a dancer and was under twenty at this time. By the time, Yerkes had mellowed and treated her better than the others.

Notes

1. *Elegant Auctioneers*, p.193.

2. op cit, p.217.

3. op cit, p.197.

4. *Sunday Tribune*, Chicago, 31 December 1905, p.3.

5. Gerber, *Alabaster Protege*, p.222.

6. Forrey, *Charles Tyson Yerkes*, p.235.

7. *Sunday Tribune*, 31 December 1905, p.1. Mrs Grigsby was lucky to escape prosecution, or did Yerkes bribe the police? He had manipulated the criminal justice system in Philadelphia and Chicago.

8. Ibid.

9. New York Society, at the top level of which were the Dutch-English families, had been intensely strict: see Edith Wharton's *The Age of Innocence*, which is regarded as an accurate depiction of 'Old New York' in the 1870s. They were known as the Four Hundred (from Burke's Peerage of the 1830s) and were suspicious of the nouveaux riches, but there were so many of them by the 1890s (the men who had made fortunes at the end of the nineteenth century, such as Yerkes) that standards began to change.

10. Hobson (1870–1937) was celebrated for his attempt to block Santiago harbour by sinking the collier *Merrimac*. He failed. He retired as a rear admiral with the Congressional Medal of Honour, and in 1942 a destroyer was named in his honour. He was deeply religious.

11. *Sunday Tribune*, 31 December 1905, p.3.

12. *Daily Tribune*, 1 January 1906, p.3.

13. *Elegant Auctioneers*, p.217.

14. Theodore Dreiser, *The Stoic*, p.3.

15. *Sunday Tribune*, 31 December 1905, p.3.

16. *Elegant Auctioneers*, pp218–9.

17. op cit,. p.218.

18. op cit, p.219.

19. The preceding quotations are all from op cit p.212.

20. Gerber, *Alabaster Protégé*, p.225.

21. *Elegant Auctioneers*, p.209.

22. op cit, quote p.210.

23. *Sunday Tribune*, 31 December 1905, p.3.

24. *Elegant Auctioneers*, pp.207-8.

25. Mrs Alec Tweedie, Thirteen Years of a Busy Woman's Life, London 1912 quote by Leonore Davidoff, 1973 *The Best Circles: Society, Etiquette and The Season*. London.

26. *Elegant Auctioneers*. p.209.

27. Ibid.

28. *Daily Tribune*, 3 January 1906, p.2.

29. Ibid.

30. Gerber, *Alabaster Protégé*, p.220.

31. *Sunday Tribune*, 31 December 1905, p.2.

32. *Daily Tribune*, 3 January 1906, p.2.

33. *Elegant Auctioneers*, p.209.

34. *New York Times*, 2 July 1911, part 8, p.1.

35. op cit, 4 July 1911, p.8.

36. *New York Times*, 6 September 1911, p.2.

37. *Elegant Auctioneers*, p.208.

38. Shane Leslie, *Long Shadows*, p.230.

39. *New York Times*, 6 September 1911, p.2.

40. Gerber, *Alabaster Protégé*, p.228.

41. Ibid.

42. *The Times*, 12 February 1964, p.15.

43. *New York Times*, 11 July 1911, p.1.

44. Ibid.

45. This paragraph is based on *Long Shadows*, pp.230-1.

46. According to John Franch in *Robber Baron*, she wrote a book, anonymously, called *I: In which a Woman Tells the Truth About Herself*. D. Appleton & Co. NY 1904. Yerkes was still alive and possibly she did not want him to know about it. Apparently it is fiction and contains a robber baron whose advances the heroine rejects.

47. W.A. Swanberg, *Dreiser*, p.166.

48. op cit, p.172.

49. *Robber Baron*, p.211.

CHAPTER SIX

THE DEATH OF THE ROBBER BARON

He died too soon.

Yerkes did not live to see the completion of his tube railways – he died from kidney disease at the Waldorf-Astoria Hotel in New York, on 29 December 1905. The hotel was a short distance from his own mansion in which his estranged wife lived. It was given out that alterations to provide for another gallery prevented him from being in his home. The Chicago *Daily Tribune* reported that there was consternation in London about the possibility of his death, which would cause confusion because the Underground was dependent on him. This was emphatically denied by Speyer, Perks and Walter Abbott of the Old Colony Trust. However, a report from London was quoted:

> When Charles Tyson Yerkes was seriously ill last summer extreme precautions were employed here to prevent the news of his condition becoming known. Everyone connected with his enterprises was instructed emphatically to deny that he was even slightly ill. The explanation was that . . . the Yerkes enterprises are so dependent on his personal genius that his death would create the utmost confusion in his properties. . . Similar rumours are again rife. [1]

By this it is meant that confidence would be undermined and shares would fall. Perks had taken the chair for him at meetings in July and August, but Yerkes presided at a difficult meeting of shareholders in

November at which some searching questions were put to him about the security of the profit-sharing notes. He was given six weeks' leave of absence by the Board. Yerkes had thought he could make London's underground railways run at a profit (an issue over which there is confusion to this day), but the venture had not, in the end, added to his fortune, instead it had tipped him into virtual bankruptcy. British investors had rightly been cautious because of the poor profit record of the District.

So, in financial terms he ended his life as a failure when he had ruthlessly striven to be a success. Given that the population of the greater London area was 8 million, he had predicted a 'financial bonanza.'[2] He said, 'In a business we always have to take chances, but I believe this is the best chance I ever took.'[3]

The Underground Board minuted their regret at their Chairman's death, and one director, Walter Abbott, reported having received 'numerous' letters of condolence. Yerkes' obituaries, in *The Times* and *The Tramway and Railway World*, were tastefully euphemistic to the point of rendering him unrecognisable (they generally are). The former said that 'like other men of distinguished energy and ability he was modest and unassuming in his private life'.[4] The latter said that he was a 'most agreeable man to do business with', and that his tastes were 'ascetic'.[5] The concluding remarks in their leading article are worth quoting:

> Personally Mr Yerkes impressed those who knew him with his real business ability, energy, perseverance, and, especially, coolness. So far as his public appearances went, he appeared to dwell in a perpetual calm; his mind seemed to have reached the ideal state inculcated but seldom reached by the Stoics, and at the same time this stoicism, instead of repressing energy and enterprise, seemed to feed it. We shall not speedily look upon his like again.[6]

Theodore Dreiser may have read this and got the idea for the title for the last book in his trilogy based on Yerkes, *The Stoic*. Yerkes' private life was tastefully concealed in London and so British sources are kinder to him than his fellow countrymen. For example, a paper by produced by the Chicago Historical Society doesn't pull any punches and called him 'the grandest robber-baron Chicago had ever seen, a five-star, aged-in-oak, 100-proof bastard'.[7]

In the summer of 1905 Emilie nursed Yerkes through his near fatal attack of nephritis. When his terminal illness started later that year and his doctors advised him to return to America, she also returned, separately, to New York. Yerkes moved in to the Waldorf-Astoria Hotel on Fifth Avenue, as did his grown-up children who had never met their stepmother, Mara.

Here, Emilie devotedly shared the work of the nurses day after day. She was now twenty-six. Mara, who knew about 'that Grigsby woman' as she called her, refused to visit him. She was not far away, in the mansion, but it was rumoured that she was afraid to leave the building in case she was locked out on Yerkes' instructions. Under pressure from his children she relented, but encountered Emilie just as she was about to leave. Dramatically, this resulted in an altercation outside the dying man's door and Emilie was escorted from the hotel. Emilie was at a disadvantage – the mistress had to defer to the wife and she never saw Yerkes again. As a result of the encounter at the Waldorf-Astoria, Mara said that she would not permit Yerkes' body to be laid to rest at their home (although in the event it was smuggled in). The funeral was symbolic; the coffin was preceded by two carriages filled with security officers and followed by six beneficiaries of the will 'with scarcely a tear of genuine sorrow shed – not even by the family'.[7] Ethel's father, Clarence Yerkes, turned up disguised as a farmer because he was on the run from the New York police. But the disguise was unconvincing and the security staff would not admit him to the mansion. Charles Tyson Yerkes was buried in the ostentatious mausoleum which he had built for Mara and himself at the Greenwood Cemetery in Brooklyn.

Emilie and the Will

Towner says that by 'complicated machinations' the great fortune melted away and it was doubtful if any one person ever understood why. 'By a system of magic that only an unraveling of the Chicago traction tangle could explain, the street railway bonds were reduced to a fraction of their value'[8] or, in other words, 'As he looted in life, so was his estate looted after life'.[9] It was the same with the other assets – they were all consumed by creditors and lawyers. By 1909 the pendulum of public opinion, after hostile publicity, had swung in Emilie's favour – at any rate in the view of the Chicago *Daily Tribune*. In a report headlined 'Widow Penniless; Ward Rich', it was said that whilst Mara lay ill in the Yerkes mansion (and there only by permission of the Receiver), Emilie, the 'beautiful ward' gave a dinner in the 'white granite palace' in Park Avenue. It went on to say that 'Her future is roseate, even more so, than during the life of her patron'. Mara, it was reported, had challenged the legality of the gifts made to her by Yerkes, but lawyers had said that Emilie's rights were 'unassailable'; and her fortune was estimated to be $2 million to $4 million.[10] This dinner party may have been her swansong in New York. The contents of the mansion were put up for sale in 1912. The Park Avenue mansion was put up for sale in 1911.

As a prominent and successful businessman, Yerkes had had some influence with newspaper editors and had managed to suppress some of his private life, though according to Towner the Chicago tabloids printed pictures of his mistresses in the 1890s. However, immediately after he died in December 1905, the American papers felt free to release the stories they had filed away and a 'decade's backlog inundated the public'.[11] After discussing Yerkes' will, the newspapers turned their attention to Emilie.

This we have already noted. It depended on who the journalists spoke to, for as Gerber says, their reports were diverse mixtures of fact and nonsense:

Emilie was socially ambitious, or she was a recluse in the mansion Yerkes gave her; she was Yerkes natural daughter, or she was merely his latest acquisition; she was the model for a Henry James heroine; she was hopelessly consumptive; she was lamed for life from a freak accident at a dinner party; she was chief legatee of a secret Yerkes will.[12]

To avoid the possibility of legal proceedings, the *New York Times* described her as his 'ward'. As already mentioned, Harpers decided not to publish *The Titan* for fear of legal action by Emilie, and several other publishers refused it. Eventually, the New York office of the British publisher John Lane decided to take the risk and the novel appeared in 1914.

Emilie's immediate reaction to Yerkes' will is unrecorded. Neither she nor any of his mistresses were mentioned in it, with the one exception was Ethel Link Yerkes, reputedly his favourite in the last year of his life, who could pass as a relative. Towner calls the will 'a veritable insurance policy for immortality' because of this.[13] Other sources, including Dreiser, say that Yerkes did not want to expose Emilie, so that there may have been some truth in the cheque story explained later. But the *New York Times* printed a report saying that Yerkes had wanted to make a new will to include Emilie because they had retained a strong affection for each other in the last weeks of his life. He kept calling for her, and she had nursed him through his illness in the summer in London. Yerkes' doctor (who was the source of this story) had reluctantly, because he was dying, allowed him to be visited by a lawyer, but when the new will was ready two days later, Yerkes was too weak to sign it. He died soon afterwards. There was then an argument as to whether this was true or not.[14] The previous day the Chicago *Daily Tribune* reported, under the headline 'Emilie Loses Last Trick', that Yerkes had given her a post-dated cheque for $250,000 shortly before he died. But according to this report the cheque was 'useless'. It was said, 'There are hints that the traction man had decided to break with her', and in the event of recovery would have stopped the cheque.[15] According to Towner she presented this cheque to the trustees, backed by her lawyers, but with what success is not known.

Yerkes had made a will in February 1904, when he was in Chicago on a money-raising visit. He was returning to London in a hurry, and signed it on the train to New York – the fabulous Twentieth Century Limited. However, on looking it over later he decided on minor changes. His faithful valet had been overlooked and was to be included. Most bequests were unchanged and the new will was witnessed in London and New York in May 1905.

The main provisions of the will were for the Fifth Avenue mansion to be his wife's home for life; it was then to become an art gallery. There was to be a hospital in the Bronx which would provide free treatment, regardless of income or race. Bequests were made to Yerkes' son and daughter (by his first marriage), together with old friends and servants – this included his personal secretary, Louis Owsely. Finally, there was money for the observatory at Wisconsin. The document achieved a 'high moral character', in Towner's words, by keeping out the mistresses.[16] One wonders if Yerkes felt guilt at all the pain he had caused his wife. *The American* said, 'Despite years of bitter separation, a post-mortem shower of gold is poured upon the widow.'[17]

When auctioned, the mansion did not reach its reserve price of $1.4 million; it sold at the second attempt for $1.2 million to a financier who said he was not going to live in it. According to the *New York Times* it was 'offered in proceedings brought by Electric Railways of London' (the Underground Group), which needed to obtain the money Yerkes had owed it.[18] His sculptures, paintings, and objets d'art attracted unprecedented attention and netted $2,207,866 – a record amount up until the 1970s.[19] The Underground directors had a legal duty to claim on the estate for the unpaid shares and these proceedings lasted four years. By 1912 his New York estate (there was a separate Chicago estate) was reported as being worth $2 million, with bequests to Ethel Link Yerkes of $40,372, Louis Owsley of $25,000 and Chicago University totalling $50,000. The City of New York gave up attempts to acquire the art collection, which went by auction to private collectors.[20] It was announced that the hospital would not be built.

The newspapers had expected Yerkes to provide well for Emilie. In fact, he did, in that she had ownership of the Park Avenue mansion together with its collection of art treasures (these were listed by the *New York Times* of 14 December 1911, p.10, prior to the sale). She had a portfolio of stocks and shares and she also possessed the jewellery he had given her (which she valued at $800,000). Additionally, Gerber says that in 1907 she started legal action against the Central Trust Company (the trustees of Yerkes' will) for 47,000 Underground shares and bonds; she may have been making a claim on the profit-sharing secured notes (or Trust Securities) which were redeemable in 1908. What this claim was based on and whether it was successful or not may be recorded in the company's records. According to Towner it was successful.

Ethel Link Yerkes arrived from Dresden and told reporters, 'Oh, Uncle was just the finest greatest-hearted man in the world' and then hurried off to the Central Trust Company to stake her claim.[21]

The Summing Up

Yerkes had two virtues – his generosity to his family and friends, and his complete lack of hypocrisy; he always said he was out for himself and himself alone, in contrast to other robber barons and politicians who said, and say, that their self-enriching antics are for the benefit of their fellow men. Another epitaph is from Burton J. Hendrick, 'In spite of the crimes which Yerkes perpetrated in American cities there was something refreshing and ingratiating about the man.'[22] Although the moral condemnation is fully justified it must be remembered that his Chicago venture was a success in business terms; he made a great deal of money which is why he was able to convince financial backers when he came to London.

It is worth reproducing an extract from Philip L. Gerber's introduction to *The Titan* by Theodore Dreiser, where he explains how and why Yerkes was of interest to Dreiser:

Many tycoons of the gilded age made – and kept – more money than Yerkes, spread a tighter net of monopoly, and were even more ruthless in their chicanery, but Yerkes possessed all the essential traits. Born with a talent for getting money, he said good-bye to books at an early age in order to engage the world of practical affairs at one; he was intuitive in discerning opportunity, and he seized upon his chances without hesitation. He understood that a tight grip on a public service would set him on the surest, fastest route to wealth, that his personal ambitions must never capitulate to any sentimental urge to consider the public welfare, and that the subornation of elected officials essential to his plans might be accomplished with an ease verging on the farcical. He was convinced that money would purchase not only men and possessions, but immortality as well; rather than a library or a college, he would leave to posterity a giant telescope, an art museum, a charity hospital, each stamped with his holy name. In addition, and unlike so many of his cohorts, Yerkes had led an uninhibited private life. Behind the flimsiest curtain of propriety, he lived unchained by the rage for respectability that reduced most financiers' lives to dull routine. He wanted as much as the next man to be both rich and well thought-of, but his personal satisfactions came first. Money being at least as much fun to spend as to earn, Yerkes lavished his millions arrogantly. . . Yerkes was not worse than other rich men, only less hypocritical.[23]

The *Dictionary of American Biography* says, realistically, of his London financial ventures:

Things did not go entirely well, however, and although he was still planning to build the greatest system of urban transportation in the world, he was a broken old man, sailing close to bankruptcy when he died in 1905.[24]

He left shareholders indignant and impoverished. For five years after his death, the estate of Yerkes was contested and wrangled over: 'By a system of magic that only an unravelling of the Chicago traction tangle could explain, the street railway bonds were reduced to a fraction of their value.'[25] When Yerkes died, he had 32,000 £10 shares in the

Underground for which he had paid £5 each. This meant he owed them £160,000 or $800,000 (approximately £10.5 million in today's values). The company made calls on his estate for the balance of £5 on each share in July 1906 and January 1907, without success, and had to resort to legal action. Judgement was obtained against his estate in January 1910; there was nothing left but the mansion and the art collection. The United States District Court appointed a receiver into whose custody they passed. Mara retreated to upstairs rooms whilst the receiver's agents made an inventory. Under a settlement agreement she was entitled to a share of the proceeds. The 300 paintings were removed to the American Art Association's galleries in Madison Square and they were sold by public auction in April 1910. Payment with interest was made to the Underground Company in early 1912.

Undoubtedly he had striven to obtain a monopoly in London – which would have enhanced the value of Underground shares considerably – but he was thwarted by the Metropolitan Railway, the City & South London and the Central London, together with tram operators and motor bus companies. His greatest miscalculation was to grossly underestimate how capital-hungry tube railways were and to overestimate the amount of traffic that electrification would generate, especially on the District railway.

Nevertheless, it is no exaggeration to say that he was a driving force in the revolution of London's railway transport in the first years of the twentieth century. At the end of the decade four new tube railways were open – three of them built by Yerkes. He was the hinge between the age of steam traction on urban railways and electric traction. His achievements, by any reckoning, were considerable – who else would have got the Metropolitan District railway electrified and three tube lines built? One cannot but agree that Lots Road power station remains as his monument, 'the symbol of his determination to unify and determine the shape of London's passenger transport'.[25]

Yerkes overcame what he saw as resistance and inertia, and complained about the general conservatism. Like many Americans he saw England as an 'old' country and its business methods as archaic. He said to American reporters:

England today is suffering from stagnation among the agricultural and lower classes...The English manufacturers do not use modern machinery...The merchants are lethargic. From Friday noon until Monday noon in England it is almost impossible to transact business...They cannot keep away from the golf links and the cricket fields on holidays, and the well-to-do all go out of town for the week's end.[26]

Unfortunately, there is more than a grain of truth in this, though Yerkes possessed no understanding of nineteenth-century English history. Possibly the greatest indictment of him is as a human being is not his morals, nor his selfishness, but his complete philistinism.

In the country that invented the railway, and when British engineers went on to build railways all over the world, it seems incredible that most of London's railways had to be engineered and financed by Americans. Awareness of this caused resentment: Britain had lost its technological lead since the first Industrial Revolution, and there was much anti-American sentiment in the media. Yerkes frequently referred to the resistance and hostility that he encountered. An unintended consequence of American electrification of the District railway on the third rail system was that this system was subsequently applied to the main line railways of southern England. Competition between private sector railways led to wasteful duplication; if the Metropolitan and the District railways had merged, not only would the quarrel about electrification have been unnecessary, but the people of London would have been better served.

Notes

1. *Daily Tribune*, Chicago, 28 December 1905, p.2. The Waldorf-Astoria was demolished in the 1930s and the Empire State Building constructed on the site.
2. Gerber, *Dreiser's Financier*, p.367.
3. Ibid.
4. *The Times*, 1 January 1906, p.9.
5. *T&RW*, 6 January 1906, p.3.
6. Ibid.
7. F.K. Plous, undated photocopy in Box 262 YER, London Transport Museum.
8. *Elegant Auctioneers*, p.229.
9. Owen Covick, R.W. Perks, C.T. Yerkes and private sector financing, p.17.
10. *Daily Tribune*, 24 April 1909, p.2.
11. Gerber, *Alabaster Protege*, p.218.
12. op cit, p.219.
13. *Elegant Auctioneers*. p.187.
14. *New York Times*, 4 January 1906, p.1.
15. *Daily Tribune*, 3 January 1906, p.2.
16. *Elegant Auctioneers*, p.187.
17. quote in *Elegant Auctioneers*, p.188.
18. *New York Times*, 12 April 1910, p.1.
19. Gerber, *The Financier Himself*, p.113.
20. The collection included Turner's Rockets and Blue Lights (1840) which hung in Yerkes' London office. On his death it was auctioned in New York with the rest of his collection. He had paid $78,000 for it; at auction it fetched $129,000. It was later restored in America so incompetently that one of the steamboats disappeared. Following an investigation by an American art historian, the damage was repaired. *Sunday Telegraph*, 17 July 2005, p.9.
21. *Elegant Auctioneers*, p.228.
22. Burton J. Hendrick, *The Age of Big Business*, p.126.

23. Gerber, *The Titan*, pp vi–vii.
24. *Dictionary of American Biography*, 1936, p.611.
25. *Elegant Auctioneers*, p.229.
26. *History of London Transport*, Vol. II, p.107.
27. Gerber, *The Financier Himself*, p.116.

CHRONOLOGY

Main Events in the Public Life of Yerkes

25 Jun. 1837	born in Philadelphia
1854	leaves school and starts work in a broker's office
1859:	marries Susanna Guttridge Gamble
1861	opens brokerage house in Philadelphia; starts collecting art
1871	defaults and imprisoned
1872	released and re-established
1873/74/75	leaves Philadelphia for Dakota – consolidates wealth
1881	divorces Susanna and marries Mary Adelaide Moore (Mara)
1881/82	moves to Chicago
1882–99	modernises urban transport in Chicago; starts second art collection
1892	purchases telescope for University of Chicago
1893	loans art collection to Chicago Exhibition
1896	visits London
1898	visits London; possibly meets R. W. Perks
1899	sells up in Chicago and moves to New York
Jun. 1900	Central London tube opens
Nov./Dec. 1900	buys control of Charing Cross tube
Mar. 1901	buys control of District, with Brompton & Piccadilly tube
Jul. 1901	forms Metropolitan District Electric Traction (MDET)
Jul. 1901	proposes takeover of Metropolitan

Jul./Aug. 1901	visits Hungary and Italy to inspect Ganz system
Sep. 1901	attacks Metropolitan in letters to *The Times*
Oct. 1901	forms Union Construction Co.
Nov. 1901	advocates direct current system at arbitration tribunal
Nov. 1901	buys Great Northern & Strand to join Brompton & Piccadilly (GNBP)
Nov. 1901	MDET buys Charing Cross from Yerkes
Feb. 1902	offer to supply Metropolitan with electric current rejected
Mar. 1902	MDET acquires partly-built Baker Street & Waterloo tube
Mar. 1902	construction of Lots Road power station starts
Mar./Apr. 1902	Edgar Speyer backs Yerkes
Apr./May 1902	forms Underground Electric Railways of London
Apr. 1902	construction of GNBP starts
Jul. 1902	conversion of District track starts.
Sep. 1902	gains control of London United Tramways and outwits J.P. Morgan
Jun. 1903	District opens first electric service on Ealing & South Harrow
Mar. 1903	construction of Baker Street & Waterloo resumed
Mar. 1903	elected Chairman of LUT
Sep. 1903	construction of Charing Cross tube starts
Jan. 1905	Metropolitan opens electric service to Uxbridge
Jan. 1905	District runs unsuccessful trial trip on Inner Circle
Feb. 1905	takes over chairmanship of District
Jul. 1905	electrified services on Inner Circle start
Aug. 1905	resigns Chairmanship of LUT due to ill health
Aug. 1905	electrified services to Ealing, East Ham, Richmond, and Wimbledon
29 Dec. 1905	dies in New York
Mar. 1906	Baker Street & Waterloo (Bakerloo) opened
Dec. 1906	GNBP (Piccadilly) opened
Jun. 1907	Charing Cross (Northern) opened

YERKES AND THE ROYAL COMMISSION

The Royal Commission on London Traffic sat from 1903–05. It had been called in the wake of the Yerkes versus J.P. Morgan clash, which aroused fears that London's transport system was being carved up by American robber barons (it was). Yerkes gave oral evidence on 18 and 24 March 1904.[1] Like many witnesses he also submitted written evidence.[2] He could look at London's traffic problems objectively; laudably, he was strongly in favour of the assessment of new railway schemes by professional railwaymen. In his written evidence he said:

> The great failures of very nearly every nature in intramural lines, whether they are municipal lines or lines owned by private corporations, can always be to lack of information or ignorance of the subject. It is like every other business at which long apprenticeship must be served to give one knowledge, and it is impossible to attain that knowledge without that apprenticeship.[3]

He then had a dig at the Commission itself:

> This makes the work of the Royal Commission particularly difficult, for the reason that there are few trained people of whom possession can be had.[4]

Predictably, Yerkes advocated that the public would gain by the formation of large corporations (subject to regulation, he assured the members) which would finance and run the underground railways of London (the

Metropolitan Railroad of New York being an amalgamation of fifteen lines). Ahead of his time, he also wanted to introduce fare zones. He ends his memorandum in philanthropic mode:

> The acme of railway transportation in the City of London and its suburbs would be that a person could travel from any one point to any other point, making connections from one line to another, all for a single fare. That would be the perfection of travel, and it will never come about unless there is an amalgamation of the railways. Heretofore London has been doing its best to keep people in some particular zone. There has been no encouragement for them to get from that zone. I may say that I have had as much experience as anyone in connection with this part of intramural transportation, and my whole desire has always been not only to build up the suburbs, but to induce the working classes to go there; consequently on the roads which I controlled in America a person could travel from the heart of the city five blocks away where the well-to-do people lived for 2 ½ d, and for the same fare could continue his ride ten miles further, which took him out on the prairie. . . What London needs for its working classes is fresh air and green grass, and they will never get either with the railways and tramways in the condition that they are at the present time, or being run as they are.[5]

In his oral evidence, Yerkes criticised the system of parliamentary committees in which railway engineers were cross-examined by lawyers as though they were 'on trial in a criminal court' as he put it. It must have seemed odd to an outsider, and it has been noted already that one of the reasons for setting up the Royal Commission was Yerkes' coup in defeating the Morgan tube scheme. Nevertheless, the Royal Commission's recommendations for co-ordination in planning and operation were not realised for another twenty-eight years (though the Underground Group achieved co-ordination by takeovers).

Notes

1. Royal Commission, Vol. II, Qq20112-20313.

2. op cit. Vol. III, Appendix 61.

3. Ibid.

4. Ibid.

5. op cit, p.628–29.

APPENDIX THREE

THE MONUMENT TO YERKES: LOTS ROAD POWER STATION

To supply the District and the tube lines, a power station (originally for the Brompton & Piccadilly tube) was built on the Thames at Lots Road in Chelsea on the site of Cremorne Gardens, which had been closed in the 1870s. Construction started in March 1902 and it was fully operational from June 1905. It contained innovations – it was the first all-turbine plant, with the largest turbines. These were British Westinghouse, which proved unsatisfactory and were replaced by Parsons in 1908–10 at Westinghouse's expense; the dispute was arbitrated by Alfred Lyttleton and was finally settled on appeal to the House of Lords in 1912. It was the largest power station in Europe at the time, if not the world. The British Press was sure about this. It has been called a monument to Yerkes (something of a power house himself) and was extensively modernised in the 1920s and in the 1960s. It lasted nearly a century until it was decommissioned in the autumn of 2002 and sold to a private property developer. Electricity for London Underground is now supplied by the National Grid.

The environmental and visual impact caused by Lots Road power station cannot be exaggerated, even though the river bank was becoming industrialised and was no longer aesthetically attractive. There were objections both from Chelsea residents and nationally,[1] it was the size and the towering chimneys – four of them – which astonished Londoners. It was lampooned by *Punch* and called the 'Chelsea Monster'. The artist James

McNeil Whistler, who had painted this part of the Thames, campaigned against it and reputedly said that the perpetrators should be '. . . drawn and quartered'. It certainly changed the bend in the river which J.M.W. Turner had painted from Battersea Old Church (still a place of worship). He had lived near the Thames in Chelsea and had been taken out on the river by watermen several times. In 1906, when an MP suggested that sites along the Thames should be used for sculptures, *Punch* produced a cartoon showing an equestrian statue of Thomas Carlyle (who lived in Chelsea) mounted on the four chimneys. But the protest evaporated and by the Second World War it had become a landmark, so much so that it was used as a symbol of resistance to the Blitz in a propaganda poster called 'The Proud City' (which quotes Whistler's allusion to a campanile). It features in great literature – in Graham Greene's *The Ministry of Fear*, also set in the Second World War, one of the characters throws a piece of bread over the wall of Chelsea embankment, and:

> . . . before it had reached the river the gulls had risen: one out-distanced the others, caught it and sailed on, down past the stranded barges and the paper mill, a white scrap blown towards the blackened chimneys of Lots Road.[2]

Chapman and the Underground Group had taken a functional view; the building was a factory for the production of a commodity, and consequently there was no need for ornamental and decorative features. For some time it has had just two chimneys, but it will not be demolished.

Notes

1. Much of Chelsea was a working-class district until the 1880s when it started to become popular with artists. Cremorne Gardens had become disreputable and protest by local residents suceeded in getting their licence withdrawn.
2. Penguin edition, 1963. p.97.

THE COLLECTOR

The British Library possesses a book about Yerkes' collection of oriental carpets, which was published in 1910. It also has two catalogues of his collection of paintings and sculptures. One is an auctioneers catalogue for the sale in 1912 of the 'valuable art and other property' from the Yerkes collection. This must have been the leftovers that did not sell at the earlier sales. The other is dated 1904, the year before he died, and is, presumably, of the complete collection as it stood at that time. It is a lavish production, bound richly in gold and green leather and printed on thick vellum-type paper. It is in two volumes, of which 250 copies were made (each copy being numbered) and printed by A. W. Elson & Co. of Boston. Yerkes has written an introduction:

In bringing this catalogue before my friends I do so with much hesitation, mainly on account of the great difficulty which all collectors have in naming the artists who have painted the pictures. Where the signature of such artist is not on the picture there can be no certainty of its authenticity unless there is direct evidence of some one who has seen it painted and has also communicated such evidence to people who have lived after him; and even where the name is so found on the picture it is possible that it may have been placed there by someone other than the artist, and fraudulently. Then, again, there are many painters who never sign a picture, and we are left to the opinion of the so-called expert, whose testimony is, to say the least, doubtful. Therefore while I have taken the best evidence at hand for the authentication of my pictures, it must not be understood that I am sure that the names attached to them are the correct ones. Where I have had grave doubts myself I have so designated, and only placed the name where I felt it was quite certain to be correct.

The two volumes contain reproductions of 208 paintings and eight sculptures in total. Each is accompanied by a brief description of the artist and his work. Presumably, these are written by an art historian who was possibly Yerkes' curator. As Wesley Towner points out in *The Elegant Auctioneers*, Yerkes' collection consisted of both famous and obscure (i.e. valueless) paintings. In the former category one would include the four Turners, four Rembrandts, five Corots, one Reynolds and one George Romney. Interestingly, there are two portraits of Yerkes, one by a painter called Jan van Beers, in which the subject is sitting at an elegant table in front of a landscape painting, looking rather like a cultured bank manager with whom one could safely leave one's life savings. The second one was done in London (the Thames is in the background) and is not flattering; Yerkes is older and overweight, with a fierce and puffy expression. This may have been done in the summer of 1905 when his terminal illness had started. The painter was Jean Joseph Benjamin-Constant. There is also a painting of Mrs Yerkes (Mara) and the description says 'sitting on a rustic bench in a park. . . A bright smile illumines her face'. Poor Mara; it is a ridiculous painting which would have been laughed at in London society.

So what was the purpose of the catalogue, which must have been expensive to produce? Undoubtedly Yerkes wanted to boast and gain the attention of art history circles; he was bequeathing the collection to the City of New York (and it is a great pity that the collection has not ended up in the Metropolitan Museum of Art in New York). Possibly most collectors had catalogues and maybe they bought and sold amongst themselves. His concern about forgeries in his introduction is interesting, as they did not have the technology that now exists with which to detect them.

THE DREISER NOVELS

As already mentioned, there are the three novels by Theodore Dreiser based on Yerkes' life: *The Financier* (1912), *The Titan* (1914) and *The Stoic* (1947). They are called, somewhat sensationally, the *Trilogy of Desire*. Dreiser's fascination with Yerkes seems to rest on some Darwinian theme. Swanberg, one of Dreiser's biographers, quotes him as saying, '... if he [Yerkes] was cruel he was also the fittest and therefore entitled to survive'.[1] It is known that Dreiser took some pains to research Yerkes' life, even to the extent of travelling to Europe. He interviewed many people who had known Yerkes, and collected newspaper articles and reports. The novels are more accurate than was originally thought. Michael Robbins says in the *History of London Transport* that it is '... very difficult at this distance of time to winnow Dreiser's fiction from fact: but much rings true'.[2]

Frank Algernon Cowperwood, based on Yerkes, is the hero of the novels: 'handsome, forceful, and dominant'. *The Financier* deals with his early life and his first career in Philadelphia including his imprisonment. *The Titan* covers his second marriage and move to Chicago, and the financing and construction of the Loop. These first two books in the trilogy had poor sales, which partly explains the long delay in producing *The Stoic*. This last novel is of relevance to London because it deals with his encounter with London's underground railways (though the reason for the title is tenuous). The dialogue seems stilted and unconvincing, but as Philip Gerber says in the introduction, it is all we have and is 'infinitely better than nothing.'[3] Unsurprisingly, the book received hostile reviews. The sequence of recognisable events for Dreiser's recognisable characters is as follows.

At the start of the novel Cowperwood has made his fortune out of the Chicago Loop, but has gone too far in his blatant bribery of the city aldermen. Enraged citizens have forced them, at gunpoint, to refuse a further franchise and Cowperwood needs to leave the city. He is therefore looking for new outlets for his financial acumen and wants to regain his social standing. He also wants to get away from his second wife – here called Aileen and based on Mara, who is living in their Fifth Avenue Mansion in New York. Cowperwood, who requires individual freedom and strives ruthlessly to get it, is also trying to divest himself of a lover, Arlette Wayne, because he is starting an affair with the beautiful Berenice Fleming (Emilie Grigsby). Berenice (whom he calls 'Bevy') suggests that he move to London. Cowperwood recalls that he had been approached in New York by two 'adventuring' Englishmen, Philip Henshaw and Montague Greaves, who 'carried letters from several well-known bankers and brokers of London and New York, establishing them as contractors who had already built railroads, street railways, and manufacturing plants in England and elsewhere'.

Henshaw and Greaves have established the Traffic Electrical Company, the aim of which is to construct a tube railway from Charing Cross to Hampstead. This has been authorised, the bill having been steered through Parliament by a firm of solicitors called Rider, Bullock, Johnson & Chance, 'as technically well-informed a combination of legal talent as the great Empire's capital could boast'. Most of the available capital has been used up in legal fees etc, and the problem now is raising more money with which to start construction.

Cowperwood sends a subordinate to London to assess the potential of this scheme i.e. the possibility of a bigger system with lines into new suburbs, and to assess the type of neighbourhood, geological formations, what exactly has been authorised by Parliament and who the shareholders are. The subordinate (called De Sota Sippens) arrives in London and what strikes him is the fact:

> . . . that in connection with the two oldest undergrounds – the Metropolitan Railway and the District railway, or Inner Circle, as it was called – there was a downtown loop, similar to that which had made the Cowperwood system of Chicago so useful to himself and so irritating and expensive to his

rivals. These two London lines, the first of the world's undergrounds, both badly built and operated by steam, actually enclosed and reached all of the principal downtown points, and so served as a key to the entire underground situation. Paralleling each other at a distance of about a mile, and joining at the ends in order to afford mutual running rights, they covered everything from Kensington and the Paddington station on the west to Aldgate in the Bank of England district on the east. In fact everything of any importance – the main streets, the theater district, the financial district, the shopping district, the great hotels, the railway stations, the houses of Parliament [sic] – was in this area.

At least we have here a new and original slant on the underground systems – even if the geography is shaky. Rather than 'badly built', it would be true to say that they were badly maintained. The story goes on:

> Sippens was quick to learn that these lines, due to their poor equipment and management, were paying little more than their expenses. But they could be made profitable, for there was as yet apart from buses, no other such convenient route to these districts. . .
>
> Moreover, there was not only considerable public dissatisfaction with the old-fashioned steam service on these lines, but a distinct desire on the part of a younger financial element now entering the underground field to see them electrified and brought up to date.

Cowperwood still has his dreams: he wants to control the complete underground system of London, and this is enough to tempt him. If he can't buy the Charing Cross line, he will buy some other line. There is huge potential in London. A firm of brokers tries to bypass Henshaw and Greaves (who have not offered Cowperwood a controlling share – he insists on 51 per cent) and approach Elverson Johnson of the Traffic Electrical's solicitors. He is religious and '. . . small, pompous, wiry, authoritative' and 'followed for the most part, an individual course that would be most advantageous to his personal plans', but is at the same time an 'embodiment of a self-conscious religious and moral rectitude which would not allow him to err too far on the side of cunning and sheer legal trickery'. This sounds like R.W. Perks, although later in the story a Mr Leeks, 'acting Chairman of the District railway', appears. Johnson had sought to buy control of the District, but it had proved to be beyond his means; it has been impossible to raise money for the Charing Cross tube so he and others have been looking for a financier who would take it over together with the Metropolitan and the District. It is his opinion that whoever can get 51 per cent control of the underground lines 'could calmly announce himself in charge and thereafter do as he pleased with them'. Enter Cowperwood.

The novel continues true to life. He brings Aileen to London but then gets her out of the way by sending her to Paris with a male acquaintance, a playboy called Tollifer who has seen better days. This gentleman has been supplied by Cowperwood with money to spend and instructions to make himself agreeable to avoid suspicion, Berenice has travelled on another steamer with her mother. She is installed in a house just outside London near the Thames. She has charm and social graces, and makes a good impression on all who meet her.

Cowperwood decides to buy the 'Charing Cross' as a means of obtaining control of the 'loop' (in the dialogue the English characters use American words like loop). He does this by buying out Greaves and Henshaw for the £30,000 they had raised, and taking over the interest on the £60,000 consols that had been purchased. Then he deposits £10,000 (possibly in the company account) as a guarantee that he will build the line. When the deal becomes public there is outrage in the Chicago papers and hostility in other American papers, although there is a favourable reaction in Britain in such papers as the *Daily Mail*.

Cowperwood proposes to Johnson and his associates that they join him in buying out the other two companies (presumably the District and the Metropolitan) in order to unify the system. Cowperwood expounds his plan of unification:

> He dwelt especially on electrification, lighting, the new method of separate motor power for each car, air brakes, and automatic signals.

At the same time he secretly plans to set up a holding company, which would be financed from the USA. The difficulties for an American entering railway and financial circles in Britain are explained to Cowperwood. Accepting this, but undaunted, he then returns to the USA and travels round the big cities, calling on banks and trust companies in order to raise money. In Baltimore he starts an affair with a great-niece called Lorna Maris (aged twenty and based on Ethel Link Yerkes). So enraptured is he that he postpones his return to London. However, hostile publicity in the gossip columns brings him to his senses and he breaks with Lorna, and returns to London with Aileen. Berenice, of course, forgives him.

Cowperwood sets up a holding company called Union Traction Underground Ltd, which will control the District, the Metropolitan [sic], and the Charing Cross tube. It will secretly buy the Baker Street and Waterloo, and the Brompton and Piccadilly. The financial arrangements allow Cowperwood 51 per cent of the stock and guaranteed interest at 5 per cent. He also takes an option on 10 per cent of the preferred Charing Cross stock, together with 10 per cent of any shares of any additional subsidiary.

Yet another holding company is formed called Railway Equipment & Construction. This has 'dummy directors and chairmen' [sic], and Johnson starts buying shares in a variety of names, resulting in a 'veritable landslide of investors descending on Cowperwood.' One takes this to mean that there is a strong demand for the stock. At this point Stanford Drake (based on J.P. Morgan) enters the fray, and a financial tussle ensues which Cowperwood wins by duplicity.

Cowperwood boasts that he will carry 200 million passengers per year with one class at a '5 per cent fare' (whatever that means), on a fully connected system providing rapid transit, and a frequent service. He is now prospering so much that he buys Turner's Rockets and Blue Lights for $78,000 (which Yerkes bought for that sum).

However, things start to unravel on the home front: Tollifer is exposed to Aileen in Paris, and she is intensely angry with her husband's deception. She returns to New York and sends Cowperwood a telegram threatening to expose him. Meanwhile Berenice is introduced to the Queen at Cowes whilst she is a guest on Lord Stane's yacht. She stands by Cowperwood whilst he weathers the storm with Aileen. On his return to New York Cowperwood tells reporters that he expects to have the London underground electrified by January 1905 and that he is building the biggest power plant in the world (the date on which he is supposed to say this is not given – in fact there are few dates in the novel). For good measure Cowperwood has purchased more paintings – a Reynolds, another Turner, and a Frans Hals. Aileen relents because she wants to be able to live in the mansion. Cowperwood now pays off Lorna.

He returns to London looking very tired and goes on a cruise to Norway with Berenice, from which he comes back refreshed. He continues to try and raise $185 million (perhaps in London) and have 140 miles of track by January 1905 (whether this means laid or modernised is unknown).

After collapsing at a party, a severe kidney condition, Bright's Disease, is diagnosed and the doctors give Cowperwood only a year to live. He decides to make a will and has a joint tomb for Aileen and himself constructed in a New York cemetery. He buys more paintings for his art gallery which he ships to New York. Lord Stane praises him for having raised $25 million from US investors, but the illness has to be concealed to prevent loss of confidence in the stock. Cowperwood's New York friend and physician is summoned to London, and tells him to rest. Cowperwood agrees to do this, but also says:

> . . . some of these concerns are not so easy to drop as you may imagine. They concern the interests of hundreds of people who have put their complete faith in me, besides millions of Londoners who have never been able to travel beyond the limits of their own neighbourhoods. With my plan, they will be able to ride to all parts of London for as little as tuppence, and so get a fairly good idea of what their city is like.

He returns to New York but his condition worsens on the boat, and he is taken by ambulance to the Waldorf-Astoria hotel (Aileen is angry and won't have him in the mansion). His illness is an international sensation and the directors of the London companies appoint Sir Humphrey Babbs to take his place temporarily.

Cowperwood discusses his will with Aileen; the mansion is to be an art gallery, a hospital for the poor is to be built and, of course, their tomb. Aileen feels she has never understood him and is almost ready to forgive, but on her way out she glimpses Berenice in the hotel lobby. Betrayed, and not for the first time, she decides not to visit him ever again. When Cowperwood is close to death his son and daughter telephone her but she refuses to see him. Dreiser produced a mawkish death-bed scene:

> They [the doctor, his secretary, and Berenice] waited for hours, the while they listened to his heavy breathing or periods of silence, until suddenly, twenty four hours later, as if seeking to conclude a great weariness, he stirred sharply, even half-rose on one elbow as though looking about, and then as suddenly fell back and lay still.
>
> Death! Death! There it was irresistable and bleak in the face of all of them!
>
> Frank! cried Berenice stiffening and staring as if in supreme wonder. She hurried to his side and fell to her knees, seizing his damp hands and covering her face with them. "Oh, Frank, my darling not you!" she cried out, and then drooped slowly to the floor half-fainting.

There is no date or time for this event. Perhaps readers of this kind of novel did not like dates.

Aileen refuses to have the coffin in her home, so it has to be smuggled in to avoid a scandal. There is a detailed description of the funeral. Berenice shuts herself up in her Park Avenue mansion while the press speculates as to where she is. She is attacked by one paper which calls her an opportunist. She is hurt by this:

> For as she saw herself, then and before, she was wholly concerned with the beauty of life, and such creative achievements as tended to broaden and expand its experiences.

Her solution is to go off to India and take up yoga.

Meanwhile Aileen gets nothing – the vultures descend and because of his debts and legal fees nothing is left of the Cowperwood fortune. The art treasures, including King Ludwig's bed, are auctioned to settle claims from Chicago and 'London Underground', which has put in a claim for $800,000. Aileen dies of pneumonia.

Finally, Berenice returns to New York and repents for her life of sin and takes up good works. This is not true to life but novels have to have a moral ending. Dreiser himself died at the end of December 1945 – the same month of the year as his hero Yerkes – and his wife completed the last two pages of the book.

Thus ends this novel. The real deathbed scene is better described by Forrey.[4] Dreiser provides no insights into Yerkes' financial skills, as the three books are mostly concerned, predictably, with his sexual exploits. The dialogue and details are entirely Dreiser's imagination.

Notes

1. W.A. Swanberg, 1965, *Dreiser*, p.172.

2. *History of London Transport*, vol II, p.62.

3. Gerber, *The Stoic*, p.XIV.

4. Robert Forrey, 1975, *Charles Tyson Yerkes*, p.238.

OTHER BOOKS IN WHICH YERKES MAKES AN APPEARANCE

1. *The Elegant Auctioneers*

This book is a history of fine art auctions in New York, and has a chapter on the disposal of Yerkes' collection. It is by an American, Wesley Towner, who died before he had completed his manuscript. The work was finished by Stephen Varble and published in the USA in 1970. It was published in Britain the following year by Gollancz. Although the book contains a lot of detailed information it is not annotated and there is no bibliography; the sources are newspaper articles and the staff and records of the Parke-Bernet Galleries. What other evidence has been used is therefore completely unknown, especially on this side of the Atlantic. I have used this as a source for lack of any other, but it has to be treated with caution. It is written in a racy and amusing style (Towner must have been a journalist and therefore prone to exaggeration). All that said, there is a lot of accessible information to be extracted, especially, as one would expect, on the sale of Yerkes' collection of paintings, furniture etc after his death (pp.228–42). The book also recounts and describes, as a background and run-up to this event, an outline of his career (pp.187 passim); his fine art collecting (p.195); his sexual liaisons in mid-career (p.197); his Fifth Avenue mansion (pp.199–204); his downfall in Chicago (pp.201–02); and his death (pp.220–21). The book is strongest on the repercussions of his will and disposal of his estate. Predictably, it is weak and inaccurate on Yerkes' foray into the modernisation of London's underground system.

On page 195 the fine art collecting is described by Towner:

In Brussels, Amsterdam, Paris, London, The Hague, Yerkes bought no end of pictures. He got a Clouet that had belonged to Horace Walpole –which of the three Clouets had painted it he did not enquire. What did it matter? It had hung they said, in Strawberry Hill before that dream of glory ended in the auctions. He bought four Brueghels before he learned that there were seven Flemish painters by the name of Brueghel who had painted with irreconcilable degrees of skill. The Countess de Bearn sold him a David, which turned out to be by the Flemish primitive Gerard David, not by the great French classicist that everyone admired. (That was, perhaps, an error on the credit side). But thanks to the more respectable European dealers, Yerkes brought back to Chicago some of the best Dutch paintings that had come to America: four by Frans Hals, one of them a masterpiece; two Jan Steens; four Rembrandts, all of them reasonably Rembrandtesque.

When Yerkes left Chicago, the collection was taken to New York by a Pullman train with the seats removed. At New York a caravan of horse-drawn wagons met the train and, with Yerkes in the lead, drove the canvases in a long procession to the Fifth Avenue mansion. Towner could not have been there, but contrives on page 201 to give a caustic and colourful description of the mansion:

The $5 million dwelling expanded by stages . . . but from the first it was a place to house a queen. Eventually it occupied more ground than any other palace on Fifth Avenue, and called for more superlatives. A Winter Garden, as it was called, sprawled L-shaped through the center of the plot, forming a vast inner courtyard covered by skylights and surrounded by a balcony with thirty-two white marble columns. The walls were of bark, the floors of black-and-white marble, the shrubs profuse, and to all appearances poisonous. One of them, a huge air plant- a particularly obscene travesty on nature – had leaves on a level with the balcony and roots hanging not only to the floor below but hauled together in bunches and tied with cords, like portieres. The fountains were simulated springs trickling from various heights over moss-grown rocks into brackish rivulets forming many little woodland pools. It was a sinister, ever-blooming Eden inhabited by cokatoos and toucans doomed to a dull bird heaven where the worms were served on platters and no leaf was allowed to fall. . .

There was a Louis XV room, and East Indian room, a Japanese room, an Empire room transported from France. . . The bedrooms were lined with green damask, mahogany, and onyx. There was a golden bed that had belonged to the King of Belgium and was said to have cost $80,000. The Mad King Ludwig's bed was cheaper but in some ways grander . . .

The two long picture galleries were simple and uncluttered, but the third, and largest, gallery-on the Fifth Avenue side, with an entrance from the street-boasted a marble staircase to outdo all other marble stair cases. Here were the sculptures- groups by Rodin and figures by Houdon, mingled alas! with a ghostly community of 8-foot maidens en route to the bath.

One gets the general idea. Towner probably gives more accurate detail, given the subject of his book, on the auctioning of Yerkes' estate and assets than any other source. .

2. *The Robber Barons*

This is by an American, Matthew Josephson, and was first published in 1934. It has a self-explanatory title and was written during the Depression of the early 1930s, as it was thought there would be interest in the previous generation 'who had misdirected the nation's economy and brought it to the debacle of 1929' (p.vii). It was re-published, in England, in 1962. The author explains the economic background and significance of the Civil War, and in this context traces the careers of the main protagonists: Fisk, Gould, Vanderbilt et al.

Yerkes enters the story as a 'former embezzler' (p.386). He dominated Chicago aldermen, who 'attained a depravity which made them famous

all over the world. They openly sold Yerkes the use of the streets for cash'
(p.386). He says he is quoting here from Burton J. Hendrick in *The Age of
Big Business*. Yerkes, as we know, made contracts with his own construction companies for re-building the lines, and 'issued large flotations of
watered stock, heaped securities upon securities and re-organisation upon
re-organisation' (p.386). Having reduced the system of Chicago to chaos he
unloaded it upon Peter Widener. But in this book there is no reference to
Yerkes' London venture, and little space is given to him in comparison to
Vanderbilt, Rockefeller etc. It is not sourced and there is a bibliography.

YERKES IS SUPPORTED BY A FRIEND

George Mortimer Pullman (1831–97) was an American who intro-duced a luxury railway carriage which was brought to Britain by the Midland Railway in 1873. He sympathised with Yerkes over the resist-ance he was meeting in London and therefore wrote a letter to *The Times* which was published on 11 October 1901. After reminding readers that he introduced the Pullman carriage to this country, he went on to point out that the streets are clogged with traffic and that the transport system is antiquated. Modernization is urgently needed. He explained that if:

> . . . such a man as Mr Yerkes could be found to undertake this task, it would be a godsend to London. I know it is out of the question even dreaming of his undertaking the work, but I am sure that others may be found equally energetic and resourceful who would do for London what he has done for Chicago within the past 20 years.
>
> The history of Chicago's solution of a similar problem may be of inter-est just now and I trust I may be pardoned for briefly referring to it. In the early eighties there were three tramway systems in Chicago – a cable road on the south side and horse-car lines on the north and west sides. The latter were about on a par for discomfort with the tramlines in London today – slow-going, dirty, ill-lighted and always overcrowded, morning and night. . . Fortunately the city council of Chicago had full control of the streets within a radius of five or six miles from City Hall. . .

Such was the situation when Mr Yerkes, poor financially, but rich in energy and enterprise, arrived in Chicago. Seeing the possibilities of the situation, he secured backing from New York and Philadelphia capitalists and speedily obtained control of the north and west Chicago systems. These he proceeded to remodel by the substitution of cable for horse power and meantime extending the lines to the city limits and beyond. The main or trunk lines of both systems were further strengthened by cross-town electric lines, which acted as feeders. In this manner ready access became possible to all parts of north and west Chicago, while the phenomenal growth of the city, which is unequalled in the history of the world, testified to the public appreciation of the benefits thus secured. The physical and financial difficulties surmounted by Mr Yerkes at Chicago, were I think, vastly greater than anything to be faced in London at present. Moreover in addition, he had to encounter the bitterest opposition and abuse from the Chicago Press, as well as the opprobrium of friendliness with the city council – a body whose reputation for municipal honesty was hardly of the best. . .

Surely what was possible in Chicago 20 years ago should not be impossible in London. Were Mr Yerkes 20 years younger, I should say it was indeed fortunate that he has taken up his abode here at a time when the rapid transit problem looks like forcing a solution. But before he or anybody else can master the difficulty a great deal of pioneer work must be done in the way of clearing off conflicting authorities, giving some one central authority and power to act, and then finding the man to do the work.

Pullman gave his address as the Hotel Cecil, where Yerkes was staying. Is it too fanciful and cynical to suggest that the letter was composed in collaboration with Yerkes, a fellow American, and intended to support him in the dispute with the Metropolitan over the Ganz system? *The Times* called the d.c. third rail system the 'American mode of traction', despite the fact that it is already in use on the Liverpool Overhead Railway.

WORKS CITED

Parliamentary papers in House of Lords Record Office

Evidence to Lords Committee on Charing Cross Euston & Hampstead Railway (No.1) Bill, May 1902

Evidence to Lords Committee on Brompton & Piccadilly Circus Railway (New Lines etc) Bill, April 1902

Company records in London Metropolitan Archives

Board Minutes. Metropolitan District Railway. 1900–05

Board Minutes. Metropolitan District Electric Traction. 1901–02

Board Minutes. Underground Electric Railways of London. 1902–05

Board Minutes. London United Tramways. 1901–10

Newspapers and periodicals

Daily Tribune/Sunday Tribune (Chicago)

New York Times

Railway Engineer

Railway Magazine

Railway Times

Richmond and Twickenham Times

The Times

Tramway and Railway World

Books, reports, and articles
(published in London unless otherwise stated)

Barker, T.C. and Michael Robbins, 1976. *History of London Transport.* Vol.II, George Allen & Unwin

Barnett, Henrietta, 1918. *Canon Barnett, His Life, Work and Friends,* John Murray

Blumenfeld, R.D., 1930. *RDB's Diary,.* Heinemann

Bobrick, Benson, 1981. *Labyrinths of Iron. A History of the World's Subways,* New York, Newsweek Books

Croome, Desmond F., 1999. *Yerkes and The Stoic.* Newsletter of the Friends of the London Transport Museum. No.55, January 1999

Croome, Desmond F. and Jackson, Alan A., 1993. *Rails Through The Clay,* Capital Transport

Covick, Owen. 2001. *R. W. Perks, C. T. Yerkes and Private Sector Financing of Urban Transport Infrastructure in London, 1900–1907.* mss. Flinders University, Adelaide

Crook, J. Mordant, 1999. *The Rise of the Nouveaux Riches,* John Murray

Davidoff, Leonore. 1973. *The Best Circles: Society, Etiquette and The Season*

Day, John R., 1972. *The Story of London's Underground*

Dictionary of American Biography. xx. 1936, Oxford University Press

Dreiser, Theodore, 1912. *The Financier,* Meridian edn 1995

Dreiser, Theodore, 1914. *The Titan,* Meridian edn 1995

Dreiser, Theodore, 1974 *The Stoic,* New York: Thomas Y. Crowell

Edmonds, Alexander, 1973. *History of the Metropolitan District Railway Company to June 1908,* London Transport Museum

Forrey, Robert, 1975. *Charles Tyson Yerkes: Philadelphia-born Robber Baron.* Pennsylvania Magazine of History and Biography, 99, (2), pp.226–41

Franch, John. 1997. *Charles Tyson Yerkes 1837–1905,* University of Chicago Alumni Magazine (offcut in *London Transport Museum*)

Idem., 2006. *The Robber Baron: The Life of Charles Tyson Yerkes,* University of Illinois Press

Gerber, Philip L., 1971–72. *The Alabaster Protégé: Dreiser and Berenice Fleming,* American Literature, 43, pp.217–230

Gerber, Philip L. 1971. 'Dreiser's Financier: A Genesis' in *Journal of Modern Literature,* New York pp.354-374

Gerber, Philip L. 1973. *The Financier Himself: Dreiser and C. T. Yerkes*, New York: PMLA, pp. 112–21.

Green, Oliver, 1987. *The London Underground: An illustrated history*, Ian Allan

Greene, Graham. 1963. *The Ministry of Fear*, Penguin edn

Halliday, Stephen, 2001. *Underground to Everywhere*. Stroud: Sutton Publishing

Hendrick, Burton J., 1919. *The Age of Big Business*, New Haven: Yale University

Hilton, George W., 1981. *The Cable Car in America*, Howell-North, California

Hodgson, Karyn, 1998. *Charles Tyson Yerkes: Swindler Turned Visionary Of The Tubes*, British Heritage. August/September 1998

Holmes, Richard, 1981. *The Little Field Marshall*, Sir John French

Horne, Mike. 2001. *The Bakerloo Line*, Capital Transport

Inwood, Stephen, 1998. *History of London*, Macmillan.

Jackson Alan A., 1986. *London's Metropolitan Railway*, Newton Abbott: David & Charles.

Jarvis, Adrian. 1993. *Portrait of the Liverpool Overhead Railway*, Ian Allan

Josephson, Matthew, 1962. *The Robber Barons*, Eyre & Spottiswoode

Kynaston, David. 1995. *The City of London*, Vol II Golden Years 1890–1914, Chatto & Windus

Lefevre, Edwin, 1911. 'What Availeth It' in *Everybody's Magazine*, 24, pp. 836–48

Leslie, Shane, 1966. *Long Shadows*, John Murray

Moffat, Bruce G., 1995. *The L: the development of Chicago's Rapid Transit System, 1888–1932*, Central Electric Railfans' Association

Olsen, Donald J., 1976. *The Growth of Victorian London*, Batsford

Passingham, W.J. nd, *The Romance of London's Underground*, Sampson Low, Marston

Report of Royal Commission on London Traffic 1905

Robbins, Michael, 1950. *CT Yerkes And Transport In London*. A Note. typescript mss at London Transport Museum

Roberts, Sydney I., 1961. 'Portrait of a Robber Baron: Charles T Yerkes' in *Business History Review*, xxxv (3), pp. 344–71

Rose, Douglas, 1994. *The London Underground: A Diagrammatic History*, Douglas Rose

Smeeton, C.S., 1994. *The London United Tramways.* Vol. 1 Origins to 1912, The Light Rail Transit Association

Sprague, Frank J., 1901. 'The Rapid-Transit Problem in London' in *The Engineering Magazine*, xxii, (1) pp.3–23

Swanberg, W.A., 1965. *Dreiser*, New York: Charles Scribner's Sons

Towner, Wesley. 1971. *The Elegant Auctioneers*, Victor Gollancz

Who Was Who, vol III, 1929–1940, 2nd edn, 1967, Adam & Charles Black

Wilson, Geoffrey, 1969. *London United Tramways: A History 1894–1933*, George Allen & Unwin

INDEX

Other titles published by Tempus

Sir Vincent Raven
North Eastern Railway Locomotive Engineer
ANDREW EVERETT

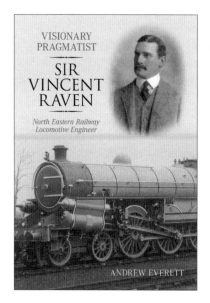

When the *Railway Magazine* of January 2000 published the results of its Millennium Poll, Sir Vincent Raven gained 42nd place, along with Thomas Newcomen and Arthur Peppercorn.

Raven's sole employer was the North Eastern railway. He rose from being an engineering apprentice at Darlington in 1878 to heading the company's locomotive and engineering department from 1910. The locomotives he designed were often visionary and ahead of their time and gave the NER a reputation for forward-thinking locomotive development.

Andrew Everett has lectured extensively on Raven and is an acknowledged expert on the subject. This is Raven's first biography, illustrated with contemporary archive photographs, portraits and ephemera, creating a cohesive biographical narrative of Raven's steam and electric locomotive building activity in the context of his life and times.

ISBN-13: 978 0 7524 3924 2

Other titles published by Tempus

Archibald Sturrock
Pioneer Locomotive Engineer
TONY VERNON

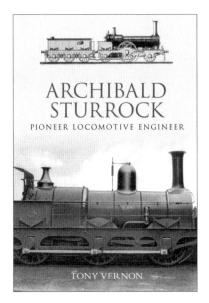

Born in 1816, by 1840 Sturrock was involved with Brunel and Gooch in establishing the Great Western Railway's works at Paddington and the new town at Swindon. On Brunel's recommendation, Sturrock was appointed locomotive engineer for Great Northern Railway, and he designed the locomotives and carriages which established East Coast main line's reputation for comfort and punctuality. He later played a lead role in establishing the Yorkshire Engine Co.

In 1863 Sturrock invented the steam tender – the predecessor of the locomotive booster – an auxiliary engine designed to give extra power at starting or at low speeds. Sturrock's later life comprised a lengthy retirement of hunting, shooting and fishing. The slightly ambiguous nature of his taking up retirement just after a costly steam tender failure has also ensured Sturrock a place as a topic for revisionist locomotive historians.

Written by his great-great-grandson, Tony Vernon, this intimate biography offers an insight into Sturrock's family and professional life.

ISBN-13: 978 0 7524 4135 1

If you are interested in purchasing other books published by Tempus, or in case you have difficulty finding any Tempus books in your local bookshop, you can also place orders directly through our website

www.thehistorypress.co.uk